THE EMMETT TILL CASE

 **MISSISSIPPI**

THE EMMETT TILL CASE

JEAN-MARIE POTTIER
TRANSLATED BY LYNN E. PALERMO

CRIME INK
CRIME INK
NEW YORK

THE EMMETT TILL CASE

Crime Ink
An Imprint of Penzler Publishers
58 Warren Street
New York, N.Y. 10007

Edited by Elsa Delachair and Stéphane Régy.
© Editions 10/18, Département d'Univers Poche, 2023
In association with So Press/Society
English translation copyright: © 2025 by Lynn E. Palermo

First edition

Cover design by Charles Perry, inspired by the French language edition cover design by Nicolas Caminade

Interior design by Maria Fernandez

All rights reserved. No part of this book may be reproduced in whole or in part without written permission from the publisher, except by reviewers who may quote brief excerpts in connection with a review in a newspaper, magazine, or electronic publication; nor may any part of this book be reproduced, stored in a retrieval system, or transmitted in any form or by any means electronic, mechanical, photocopying, recording, or other, or used to train generative artificial intelligence (AI) technologies, without written permission from the publisher.

Library of Congress Control Number: 2025935586

Paperback ISBN: 978-1-61316-692-5
eBook ISBN: 978-1-61316-693-2

10 9 8 7 6 5 4 3 2 1

Printed in the United States of America

Pastoral scene of the gallant South
The bulging eyes and the twisted mouth

"Strange Fruit," a poem by Abel Meeropol,
Sung by Billie Holiday

Contents

PROLOGUE: The Ghosts Across the Bridge 1

THE COTTON CURTAIN (1955) 9
   1. Silence and Shadows 11
   2. Mississippi Goddam 18
   3. Strange Fruit on the Tallahatchie River 26
   4. A Good Place to Raise a Boy 36
   5. The Hunt for Witnesses 45
   6. "There He Is" 57
   7. Two Mothers on the Stand 61
   8. The Home of the Brave 70

SHIFTING MEMORIES (1955–2004) 79
   9. Two Men Free and One Hanged 81
   10. Confessions for Sale 89
   11. The Dream and Its Martyrs 101
   12. "If I Did It" 115
   13. A Coffin Still Open 125

A LIFE THAT MATTERS (2004–2023) 135
   14. The Dead Speak 137
   15. Anatomy of a Murder 151

16. The Confession That Couldn't Be Found	160
17. Rashomon in the Delta	168
18. "Say His Name!"	174
19. The End of the Trail	181
EPILOGUE: The Statues' Gaze	189
APPENDICES	207
Map of the Delta Region	209
Places Related to the Emmett Till Case	211
Chronology	213
Sources	219
Acknowledgments	227

PROLOGUE

The Ghosts Across the Bridge

A twenty-ton white steel cross towers one hundred twenty feet high over a tiny park. At its base, an American flag keeps watch over a manicured lawn that clashes with the backdrop of yellowed grass and crumbling asphalt. In 2021, a religious organization had the monument built in the hope that it would inspire drivers to pray as they passed through Greenwood, the self-proclaimed "Cotton Capital of the World" in the heart of Mississippi.

Without the cross, this place would just be an unremarkable intersection, the halfway point between a car dealership and a Walmart. However, local rumor has it that it is a historical landmark. People whisper that here, on the outskirts of Greenwood in 1938 stood a grocery and juke house called Three Forks, which might be where blues musician Robert Johnson was poisoned when he swigged mothball-laced corn whiskey. Since then, one more name has been added to the criminal renown of the region facing the great white cross: Emmett Till.

In 2005, the state of Mississippi erected a blue historical marker on the gravel shoulder, naming a thirty-two-mile stretch of US Route 49 the Emmett Till Memorial Highway and paying belated respects to this Black adolescent from Chicago, fifty years after his death on August 28, 1955. Emmett Till was the victim of one of the most infamous racist crimes in the state's history.

For those who want to look for ghosts, the place is full of them. The ones relating to the Emmett Till case reveal themselves even more willingly farther from the highway. They come to meet you as you cross the two bridges north of this city of fifteen thousand. The first bridge, topped with a gray truss, marks the beginning of Grand Boulevard, an elegant avenue typical of the aristocratic South with its long vault of oak trees and white colonnaded residences.

The second bridge sits on a narrow country road bordered with forests and fields. Cotton has now ceded its preeminence to soybeans and corn. The old cabins of plantation laborers have been renovated to accommodate

PROLOGUE: THE GHOSTS ACROSS THE BRIDGE

tourists. About nine miles farther along, you reach the deserted village of Money, where you can gaze at an emblematic landmark in the history of civil rights in the South, Bryant's Grocery & Meat Market.

This shuttered grocery store would be easy to miss if it weren't for the commemorative marker out front. The place has been abandoned since the mid-1980s. Time and weather, especially Hurricane Katrina in 2005, have done their work. In the summer, the brown brick walls disappear almost entirely behind raging kudzu. The upper floor has collapsed, and the interior has been invaded by vegetation and cluttered with worm-eaten boards scattered about like pickup sticks. An orange safety barrier out front and a small sign reading PRIVATE PROPERTY. NO ONE ALLOWED ON PROPERTY, VIOLATORS WILL BE PROSECUTED in threatening red letters attempt to keep curious visitors at bay. Some of them go in anyway.

❖

Dusk was falling on August 24, 1955, when Emmett Till, on vacation with his relatives in Mississippi for a couple of weeks, arrived at this store, along with a small band of his cousins and their friends, all of them teenagers.

Money, a great misnomer, offered few possibilities for entertainment. Wedged between the Tallahatchie River and the railroad tracks, the main street was, at the time, limited to a few stores, a post office, a gas station, a school, and a cotton gin. The coffee shop the little gang of friends had in mind was closed, so instead, they headed over to the grocery store owned by Roy and Carolyn Bryant, a white couple who had lived there for two years.

On the green-and-white porch plastered with Coca-Cola ads sat a small group of young Black boys absorbed in a game of checkers, using bottle caps for game pieces. When Emmett's group arrived, some of them stayed outside to chat or comment on the players' moves, while others went into the grocery store, a few at a time, to buy a drink or candy.

Emmett Till followed Wheeler Parker, one of his cousins, into the store. Carolyn Bryant, twenty-one years old, with dark hair and pale skin, was not much older than her customers. She was working alone at the cash register, as her husband had gone off to deliver a load of shrimp somewhere between New Orleans and Texas. When Wheeler went back outside with his bottle of soda, Emmett was left alone in the store with Carolyn Bryant. A moment later, Simeon Wright, another cousin, joined him inside. His older brother,

PROLOGUE: THE GHOSTS ACROSS THE BRIDGE

Maurice, worried that Emmett might commit a breach of Southern custom.

A few minutes later, the boys came out of the store together to join their friends and the others playing checkers. After that, Carolyn also came out onto the porch. And right at that moment, everyone heard a long, provocative whistle. Twice. A whistle America had dubbed a *wolf whistle* ten years earlier, alluding to the "whee-woo" the lewd wolf in Tex Avery cartoons would emit whenever he spotted a buxom vixen, eyes wide, tongue dangling. This whistle, released in Money at dusk, had escaped the lips of Emmett Till.

As if feeling threatened, Carolyn Bryant hurried to her sister-in-law's car with determined stride to retrieve the revolver she'd left in the glove compartment that morning—a gun she had never imagined herself capable of using.

A shout of alarm went up. "She's getting a gun!" It was the signal for Emmett and his cousins to make a dash for their 1946 Ford. In his panic, one boy dropped his cigarette, which rolled under the seat of the car. The time it took for him to retrieve it before starting the car meant the loss of precious seconds on their start ahead of possible pursuers. Indeed, only a few hundred yards down the road, the teenagers could see the growing glare of headlights out the rear window, as if another car, maybe carrying Carolyn Bryant's family, was gaining on them.

They slammed on the brakes and pulled over on the shoulder, and everyone except the youngest, Simeon, who stayed huddled on the backseat, jumped out and hid as deep in the blooming cotton field as they could. False alarm: The car following them drove past without slowing.

When they got back to the family home a few minutes later, Emmett begged his cousins not to mention the incident. "Please don't tell your father I whistled at that lady." The boys agreed, afraid their parents would send him back to Chicago. But the next day, a girl in the village, who'd been part of the grocery store expedition, predicted that they had not heard the last of the offense committed against Carolyn Bryant. "I know the Bryants, and they are not going to forget what happened."

Emmett Till had three more days to live.

THE COTTON CURTAIN
(1955)

1
SILENCE AND SHADOWS

"Preacher!"

It was 2:30 in the morning on Sunday August 28, 1955, when the nickname, followed by pounding on the door, tore through the nocturnal silence. In Money, the village where Mose Wright had lived for ten years, everyone called him "Preacher" or "Preacher Wright." Even his wife Elizabeth.

For several decades, this man, who had been a conscientious objector during World War I, had played the role of itinerant preacher before founding a little parish close to home. For some, using this nickname was a sign of respect toward a man of a venerable age. For others, it was the only alternative to the paternalistic "Uncle Mose." In this region of Mississippi, which, a century

THE EMMETT TILL CASE

after the abolition of slavery, was still the most segregationist state in the United States, a white person would never have lowered himself to calling a Black man "sir."

"*Preacher*! This is Mr. Bryant. I want to talk to you and that boy."

Mose Wright had several boys staying at his house, a house built of raw wood and propped up on concrete blocks to protect it from the frequent floods from the river. The residence was modest but well-kept. The old man's landlord, a white man about seventy, born in Germany and honest in his business dealings, had lived there previously. Wright farmed about twenty-five acres of cotton for him. The preacher had been married twice and had twelve children—four daughters and eight sons. In 1955, the three youngest were still living with him: Maurice, sixteen years old; Robert, fourteen; and Simeon, twelve. But that's not who the two half brothers out on the front porch were looking for.

The first man, Roy Bryant, twenty-eight years old, with dark eyes and eyebrows, looked like a Hollywood supporting actor. He also played a supporting role in life. He earned a living, though not very well, through trucking to supplement his grocery store business located three miles from there, on the main road in Money. He and his wife Carolyn, who'd been a local beauty queen and was the daughter of a deceased plantation manager, lived with their two sons in a modest apartment behind the store.

One of Roy Bryant's half brothers, John William Milam, who went by "J. W." or "Big Milam," stood beside him on the porch. Twelve years, two inches, and even more extra pounds separated him from the younger half brother. Balding and with a thick chin, J. W. Milam operated a fleet of farm machinery and trucks in the region, driven by Black workers he ruled over with an iron fist. He also owned a gas station in the village of Glendora, about twenty miles north. Wielding a powerful flashlight in his left hand and a Colt .45 in his right, he was the one running this interrogation now.

"You have two boys from Chicago here?"

Actually, Mose Wright was housing three of them. Earlier that evening, one of his grandsons, Curtis Jones, had arrived from Illinois for a few days of vacation. A week earlier, Mose himself had returned home from Chicago with two other teenagers in tow. They'd taken the City of New Orleans, the train connecting Illinois to the South. One was Wheeler Parker Jr., aged sixteen, another grandson from the city. The other was Emmett Till, alias "Bo" or "Bobo," a grandnephew.

Emmett was the only son of Mamie Till, Mose's niece by marriage. Emmett had just celebrated his fourteenth birthday at the end of July. For him, life in Mississippi was filled with new discoveries each day. With his cheerful round face and lively eyes, he amused and sometimes scared his family with his wild antics. When he and his cousins went to buy firecrackers in Money the day after he arrived, he set off a few of them right after walking out of the store.

Mose, who was reputedly uncompromising with his sons, cast an indulgent eye on Emmett's lack of aptitude for picking cotton under a withering sun, the activity that occupied the greater part of the family's days. When they weren't working in the fields, the boys swam in the nearby ponds after chasing out the formidable water moccasins by beating them with sticks. They made gluttonous raids on the watermelon fields.

The previous evening, most of them had been out late in Greenwood, the nearest big town. Some had gone to see a western; the others, including Emmett and his elders, had wandered the streets, where men went to visit taverns for fun, gamble, and pick up girls. In Mississippi, where Prohibition was still officially in effect, they even allowed themselves a little *white lightning*, bootleg whiskey. They'd gone home to bed a little before one o'clock in the morning.

"I want the boy that done the talking down at Money."

Mose and Elizabeth Wright had not waited for this request to figure out the motive for the intrusion; they feared something like this. On Wednesday evening, August 24, when their son Maurice dropped them off at church, they warned him and the boys not to drive far. None of them had a driver's license. Their warning fell on deaf ears. Hardly had they turned their back when the boys were already on the rutted road to Money. The route was known by locals as Dark Fear Road because of the snake-infested creeks, somber woods, and forgotten murders. Eventually, the great-uncle and the great-aunt heard about the incident at the grocery store. They knew very well that J. W. Milam and his half brother had come looking for Emmett.

"If it is not the right boy, we are going to bring him back and put him in the bed."

Going through the dark bedrooms one by one, searching by the beam of their flashlight, the two men finally laid their hands on Emmett in the bed he was sharing with his cousin Simeon. Elizabeth hadn't had enough time to take her grandnephew out the back door, where he could have fled into the cotton fields. Mose kept two rifles in the house but feared a massacre if he tried to reach for them. Helpless, all he could do was wake up his grandnephew. Immediately, J. W. Milam shouted at him.

"Are you the one who did the smart talking up at Money?"

The two intruders ordered Emmett to follow them. Still half asleep, he obeyed without objecting. The great-uncle and his wife implored the two men. They would pay them whatever they wanted. The kid hadn't known what he was doing; he just needed a good spanking. Exasperated by Elizabeth's pleas, J. W. Milam ordered her to get back in bed and make sure he could hear the mattress springs squeaking as proof. He was even more threatening to Mose Wright.

"How old are you?"

"Sixty-four."

"If you know any of us here tonight, then you will never live to get to be sixty-five."

Even if he'd wanted to, Mose Wright couldn't have identified some of the figures, mere shadows who had come along with the two brothers. When Roy Bryant and J. W. Milam arrived, he'd glimpsed a third man on the front porch, where he enjoyed a pipe on lazy evenings. That person stayed outside and hid his face with his hand as if fearing he'd be recognized. But to Mose Wright, he seemed to be Black. Then, as the abductors were leaving, the old man heard another voice just before a thick and terrified silence fell over the house. It came

THE COTTON CURTAIN

from a little farther away, from inside the car or van parked with headlights out a few yards from the road, in the shadows under the low branches of two cedars and a persimmon tree. When asked if Emmett Till was the boy who had caused the ruckus at the grocery store, the voice answered with no hesitation.

"Yes."

2
MISSISSIPPI GODDAM

"If you have to humble yourself, then just do it. Get down on your knees if you have to."

"Oh, Mama, it can't be that bad."

"Bo, it's worse than that."

Before Emmett Till left on his vacation, his mother had tried to get the message through that Mississippi was not Chicago. Unlike his cousin and best friend Wheeler Parker, born just ten miles from Money, Emmett had never learned to master the codes governing relationships between Blacks and whites in the South. Mamie Till had only reluctantly let him go to the state of her ancestors three times in his life, and always escorted by herself or by one of her aunts. She protected him.

THE COTTON CURTAIN

Having become a mother nine months after her wedding at the age of nineteen, Mamie had raised Emmett mostly without his father, Louis Till, who was a worker from Missouri. A year after Emmett's birth, Mamie left Louis, who was also an amateur boxer and a sometimes-violent husband. She obtained a restraining order against him, which he violated several times. Finally, a judge gave Louis Till a choice: either prison or the Army, which at the time meant risking his neck to liberate Europe.

On July 13, 1945, more than two months after Germany's surrender, Mamie received a terse telegram from the US Army informing her that the father of her son had died. Twelve days later, Emmett blew out his four birthday candles as a fatherless child.

Mamie then lived through two other relationships with two other World War II veterans, and each of them ended in divorce. She even went to Michigan to try her luck for a while before coming back to Chicago, where she worked as a secretary for the Air Force. From then on, she lived alone with her son.

Emmett, a spoiled only child, was an ordinary little American of his era. He was an average student and an obliging boy. He never missed a Sunday at church and earned a little pocket money by mowing lawns or shoveling sidewalks in Woodlawn, one of the Black neighborhoods in South Side Chicago. Energetic and always ready to play a game, especially when he was in charge, he also loved superhero comic books, Abbott and Costello, dancing bebop, and listening to doo-wop records.

At his age, when his thoughts about possible vocations were constantly changing, he sometimes dreamed of being a professional baseball pitcher or, more realistically, a motorcycle cop. His mother imagined college studies, maybe a religious career for him. Emmett was quite tall for his age and a little chubby, but it was a different physical detail that set him apart, one left over from a violent attack of polio at the age of six. He had a persistent stutter. To fight it, his mother made him practice his diction by reciting the Constitution and the Gettysburg Address. When he got stuck on a word, she taught him this strategy: pause, whistle, then try again.

For the summer of 1955, when Emmett would be celebrating his fourteenth birthday, Mamie planned to take him on a vacation in her new Plymouth automobile, first to his grandfather's house in Michigan, then to a cousin's house in Nebraska. That was before the visit

THE COTTON CURTAIN

to Chicago by Mose Wright, Emmett's great-uncle, to officiate the funeral of a former parishioner.

While there, Mose engraved four magic syllables in the young boy's imagination: Mississippi. And not just any Mississippi, but the Delta region. The region is shaped like a football and located in the northwest part of the state. As the saying goes, it starts at the lobby of the Peabody, the fancy hotel in Memphis, and ends a four-hour drive to the south in Vicksburg on the cliffs overlooking the Mississippi River. For Emmett, these names and their vistas rang like a promise of freedom.

The names of the rivers—Yazoo, Tallahatchie, Yalobusha—all borrowed from the Native Americans after they had been forced from their lands long ago, seemed to exhale an exotic scent. In ancient times, the flooding of the Mississippi River had made this soil one of the most fertile areas in the world, like the Nile Delta. Gradually reclaimed from mosquitoes and alligators after the Civil War, it now flourished thanks to cotton. On good days, its fields were covered with millions of small white flowers, to the point where it sometimes looked like snow in the summer.

For Mamie Till, other less flowery images of the Delta came to mind. She'd been born in the region, in the village of Webb, situated twenty-five miles north of Money. Her family left Webb when she was two. In January 1924, they had joined the Great Migration, the massive exodus of Blacks from the South toward the promised lands of the North. Destination: Summit, a small suburb of Chicago.

Confronted with the shock of the floods, the voraciousness of the boll weevil, and the mechanization of the cotton industry, African Americans of Mississippi set off toward what they hoped would be a more thriving future. Chicago, where steel mills and slaughterhouses were hiring aplenty, made a favorable landing point. It also held the promise of fulfillment.

The Illinois metropolis was certainly brutal, and discrimination at work, in housing, and in recreation was common currency, but Blacks could work, live, and vote quite freely. It was not like Mississippi, where implacable systematic segregation ruled—segregation that Mamie Till rediscovered seemingly untouched each time she returned there. Mamie could shout "Mississippi Goddam" ten years before Nina Simone's anguished cry. She had never forgotten the icy reception she'd received in a store, nor her grandfather's subsequent rebuke, when at the age of twelve, she was on vacation in her tiny birth town. Her offense: crossing the main street to buy toilet paper and an ice cream cone on the "white" side. "You know what? I'm gonna give you that ice cream cone. But I am *not* going to sell you no toilet paper," the merchant had retorted. "You go on home, use corn cobs like all the others."

In late August 1955, Mamie Till was even more worried about her son because an ill wind was blowing through Mississippi. On August 13, Lamar Smith, an organizer involved in mobilizing Black voters, was shot dead in broad daylight right in front of a courthouse in the southern part of the state. Three months earlier, the Reverend George Lee, an activist from the Delta, had been gunned down in his car. In both cases, no one had been convicted of the murder.

An attentive reader of the African American press, Mamie knew that much of Mississippi was not processing the *Brown v. Board of Education* decision of the previous year, which had ordered the schools in the South to end segregation. The most enraged segregationists had warned that if they were forced to send their kids to the same schools as the Black children, blood would splatter the marble steps of the court.

Mamie wanted her son to respect the rules relating to segregation to avoid putting himself in danger—especially those rules governing his interactions with white women. If Emmett saw one, he should drop his head, not even look at her, or cross over to the other side of the street. He must never speak to white people unless spoken to. Always punctuate his answers with polite formulas, like "Yes, sir" and "No, ma'am." Be ready to apologize, excuse himself even if he didn't think he'd done anything wrong. Eager to make the trip, Emmett reassured her, saying, "Mama, I know how to act. You taught me how to act."

After hearing about his first week in Mississippi, Mamie felt a little less tense. On the telephone and through the mail, Great-Aunt Elizabeth Wright heaped praises on Emmett. On Saturday, August 27, Mamie also received a short letter from her son. Everything was going fine, he was having fun, and he asked her to have his motorbike repaired before he got home the following week. He promised to pay her back once he had a little money in his pocket. At the end of his letter, he hinted, in parentheses, that he'd spent all his cash. Apparently, the few dollars that Mamie and her companion Gene Mobley had slipped into his pocket before he left had not been enough. Feeling reassured, the mother invited a few girlfriends over for the evening, then went to bed, her mind more at peace.

THE COTTON CURTAIN

Sunday morning, the phone rang a few minutes before she was supposed to leave for church. It was Willie Mae, her cousin and the mother of the young Curtis Jones, who had taken the train the previous day to join Emmett in Mississippi. She was in tears. "I don't know how to tell you. Bo . . . Some men came and got him last night."

3
STRANGE FRUIT ON THE TALLAHATCHIE RIVER

At the moment when his abductors ordered Emmett Till to follow them, two details increased their rage tenfold. First, the young man answered with a simple "yes" when asked if he'd talked smart at the grocery store. Second, he'd insisted on slipping on socks before putting on his shoes.

Three days later, these same feet, bare this time, announced to the world the news of his death in the middle of the Tallahatchie River. Serenaded by croaking frogs and singing grasshoppers, the countryside looked peaceful, with its milk-chocolate waters filled with rotting trunks and undergrowth bordered by oaks, ash, and cypress. But it was whispered that strange fruit had

THE COTTON CURTAIN

hung from the branches in the region and the waters contained dozens of Black corpses thrown to the catfish and tortoises.

It was a teenager named Robert Hodges who found the body. On August 31, a little after six o'clock in the morning, the boy from Philipp, a village just north of Money, was gliding along in his motorboat to pull the fishing lines that he'd set out at a bend in the river when his eyes fell on a strange spectacle: a pair of legs sticking out of the water toward the sky. He sped back to tell his father and the owner of their property, who alerted the authorities.

The corpse had gotten caught on something as it floated down the river. Using a rope, the police were able to unhitch it, then reel it in to the riverbank. Seriously decomposed from the time spent in the river, the bloated body was almost greenish. His tongue was sticking out, one eye had been gouged, and the other burst, and the skull had been shattered. Tied around his neck with about fifteen inches of barbed wire was a fan from a cotton gin, the machine used to separate cotton fiber from the seed. It weighed about seventy-five pounds, but the mud from the river had almost doubled its weight. Whoever had attached it had intended to submerge the corpse forever at the bottom of the river. But their error was they'd forgotten to weigh the feet down too.

Mose Wright was quickly notified of the macabre discovery. When he arrived on the scene, they turned over the body, which was lying face down in an outboard motorboat. The old man thought he recognized him. Though he didn't know the piece of jewelry on the victim's right middle finger, his sons were categorical. Emmett had shown off the silver signet ring a few days before and even let them wear it.

Bearing the engraved inscription, "May 25, 1943, L.T," the ring had been purchased by Louis Till in Casablanca during his military service at the front and had been sent back to his widow after his death. For years, Emmett had kept the ring in a box. The few times he did try to wear it, he wound adhesive tape around it, so it wouldn't slide off his slim finger.

Before shutting his suitcase for this trip to Mississippi, he'd come across the ring while looking for cuff links and noticed it was starting to fit better. Mamie thought it was time to give him another memory of his father—maybe a medallion with a photo of him in uniform. She would make it a gift for his fifteenth birthday.

❖

THE COTTON CURTAIN

When Mamie saw Ollie Williams, her best friend, show up on her front step, she understood what had happened. Until then, she still had hope. For three days, she had been glued to the telephone, calling Mississippi again and again for information with no success. She felt like she'd run into a wall, as if her own country was divided in two, she'd say later, just like faraway Europe. Cut in two by a "Cotton Curtain" lined with steel.

She had also called on the press and civil rights militants in her city and imagined a happy ending. Who knew, maybe her son was hiding out in the woods or had found refuge at someone's house in the neighborhood. Among the people supporting her, the most lucid didn't dare tell her the truth, which she knew in the deepest part of herself. In Mississippi, Black people didn't get kidnapped, they got killed.

In Money, they were ready to bury the body immediately—and the affair along with it. The authorities in Tallahatchie County, where the body had been found, ordered that the burial take place as soon as possible, even in the afternoon of August 31. The grave had been dug in the little church cemetery where Uncle Mose Wright had preached in the past. It's also where he'd offered prayers on the evening of the grocery store incident.

Not accustomed to contesting orders from the authorities, Emmett's southern family had rung the assembly bell. But certain members notified Mamie Till, who refused to have her son buried without her and so far away. She requested that he be returned to Illinois. The state of Mississippi accepted under one condition: that the casket remain sealed.

On the morning of September 2, 1955, a large crowd that had been kept informed of events almost hour by hour converged on the City of New Orleans train as it arrived at Central Station in Chicago. It was the very place Emmett Till should have arrived home, upright and on two feet, after his two-week vacation. Mamie Till arrived at the platform in a wheelchair pushed by family members. She stood up as the baggage car pulled in, then collapsed when she saw the enormous shipping casket being unloaded. Reporters could hear her lamenting, "I would have gone through a world of fire to get you. I know I was on your mind when you died."

As it was transferred to a hearse, the casket gave off a pestilential odor, worse than a slaughterhouse. The undertakers tried to dissipate the stench with generous squirts of deodorizing spray. When she arrived at A. A. Rayner and Sons, a funeral home preferred by the Blacks of Chicago, Mamie Till was informed of the orders

THE COTTON CURTAIN

issued by the state of Mississippi that she was prohibited from seeing her son one last time. Gathering all her determination, she refused the order. She was ready to take a hammer to the coffin to break it open, if necessary.

Simeon Booker, a journalist in Chicago at the influential African American magazine *Jet*, who'd developed a relationship of trust with Mamie Till, was at her side with photographer David Jackson in this new stage of her torment. Her eyes riveted on what lay inside the coffin, Mamie autopsied her only son. Later, she would say that she was remembering the first time she'd laid eyes on him fourteen years earlier, how disfigured he'd seemed from the pain of birth.

Now that seemed derisory. Inch by inch and body part by body part, she tried to reconstruct this body she knew by heart. His skinny calves. His round knees. His genitals had not been mutilated; the killers had not performed that part of the lynching ritual. His nose was shredded, as if put through a meat grinder. His eyes were worse than extinguished; the left one had been smashed and the right one, dug out, was dangling from the socket by the optic nerve. The upper part of his right ear was missing, and there was a half-inch hole in his temple.

In her shock, Mamie Till thought she could see daylight filtering through his crushed skull, but it was cotton batting that the undertakers had slipped in to take the place of his brain. At the end of her examination, only a single question came to her, which seemed absurd, painful, and compassionate all at the same time.

"Was it necessary to shoot him?"

After detailing this monstrous tableau, Mamie Till demanded that it be made visible to all. She was not going to do, as was too often done by tearful families in similar crimes, just discreetly bury the dead relative in a corner. Others had to bear witness to what she had seen. "Let the world see what they did to my boy," she ordered.

Not only would the body be laid in an open casket with just a single pane of glass separating the living from the face of the dead, but she also gave David Jackson permission to take photographs of Emmett's body. When the employees lifted the young man's body from the coffin to place it on a display table, a piece of the skull dropped onto the floor. Stunned, Simeon Booker watched his colleague gather it up and set it in place, "calmly, like putting on a hat."

Two days later, nearly two thousand people squeezed into the Roberts Temple Church of God in Christ, the Pentecostal church Emmett Till's grandmother had joined when she'd arrived in Chicago. At least as many stood outside, ears turned to the loudspeaker that broadcasted the funeral service. Even more filed past the casket, day after day and even at night to see the adolescent's corpse. Several tens of thousands, first at the funeral home, then in the nave of the church.

After waiting in the street sometimes for hours, one after another, the pilgrims of misfortune paused and reflected before the body of Emmett, dressed in the white shirt and slightly too large black suit that he'd found under the Christmas tree eight months before. Some mourners went pale, some cried, some hid their faces so as not to see what they had seen, and some even fainted. Others went past without a gesture or a word, filled with a suppressed fury.

The reverend agreed to wait two days after the funeral services before consigning the body to the earth, giving everyone time to say their prayers. On September 6, a brief, final ceremony of farewell was held in the church. In tears, Mamie Till pleaded that, before shutting the coffin, the three photos of happier days, which she had used to line the casket, be returned to her. There was Emmett, his face serious, wearing a fedora given to him by Gene Mobley; Emmett smiling at the camera, leaning on his elbows on the television set; Emmett and his mother, with her arm around her son's right shoulder.

Then the pallbearers, six of Emmett's friends, escorted the casket to a van that headed off in the direction of Burr Oak Cemetery in Alsip, a small town in the Chicago suburbs. At the foot of the grave bordered with flowers, a young white pastor with the Roberts Temple collapsed. Mamie Till sobbed and doubled over. Her mother, Emmett's grandmother, raised an arm toward the sky, an arm sheathed in her long black glove—an arm that called for mercy, and maybe justice as well. The casket was lowered into the earth in the middle of a large grassy lawn, where a discreet plaque decorated with a photo in a gold medallion would soon be placed.

EMMETT L. TILL, IN LOVING MEMORY, JULY 25, 1941–AUG. 28, 1955.

The young man's murderers had thought they were sinking Emmett Till in the mud forever, but they'd failed. They'd thought they had disfigured him to the point of making him impossible to look at, but they'd failed. Even the burial didn't make him vanish in the eyes of the world. On September 15, *Jet* magazine published three photos of the corpse, after careful deliberation. The magazine was printed in pocket format, but the

THE COTTON CURTAIN

snapshots—one wide-view and two close-ups—exploded at readers.

Jet was one of the favorite publications of the Black community. People passed issues around their families, and copies were worn thin in hair salons and coffee shops. They reprinted the issue several times, for the first time ever. But even that wasn't enough. *Jet* republished one of the photos the very next week, and other publications followed suit.

Hundreds of people had received Emmett's casket at the train station without actually seeing his corpse. Tens of thousands had observed him with hardened or appalled looks at the funeral home and at the church. Now, hundreds of thousands of Americans contemplated his face in black and white on paper. In Louisville, Kentucky, one reader was so moved by what he'd seen that he decided to avenge the Chicago teenager in his own way. One night, with a friend, he hurled stones at a US Army recruitment poster. Like many young people his age, Cassius Clay, the future Muhammad Ali, would never forget the face of Emmett Till.

4
A GOOD PLACE TO RAISE A BOY

William Faulkner had received the offer by telegram on yellow Western Union paper. It was an invitation to a debate. The sender was the old African American activist W. E. B. Du Bois, who proposed to confront their perspectives on desegregation. Both favored it, but not in the same way. Du Bois thought Black people had already waited too long for equal rights. Faulkner, on the other hand, thought that, given the context of violence and hate in the South, desegregation would have to happen gradually and the activists would need to help keep the situation calm.

The man who, in the eyes of the world, embodied Mississippi for adding fictional Yoknapatawpha County to the map in novel after novel, had seized the opportunity to express himself on the Till case. Immediately after the body was discovered, his voice surged from Rome, where he was on the day of the crime. "If we in America have reached that point in our desperate culture when we must murder children, no matter for what reason or what color, we don't deserve to survive, and probably won't."

A little later, he shifted registers in provocative and often inebriated interviews. Of course, the murder of a child was unacceptable, but "the Till boy got himself into a fix and he almost got what he deserved." And if Mississippi continued to be harassed, it would end in war and he would take the side of his birthplace state, "even if it meant going out into the street and shooting Negroes."

Broadcast widely, his ideas created an uproar. After all the tumult, the one thing he was sure of was that he did not want the debate. Politely, he explained to W. E. B. Du Bois that he didn't want to embody the call for patience and moderation in the face of a morally unassailable position. Which was unfortunate because his opponent had thought of a good backdrop for the meeting: the front steps of the Sumner Courthouse in Tallahatchie County. The place where J. W. Milam and Roy Bryant had just been tried.

❖

The trial opened on September 19, 1955, barely three weeks after the discovery of Emmett Till's body. Seventy reporters, mostly from outside the state, had made the trip to Sumner. The major news agencies, the daily newspapers, and the national magazines were there. Television channels had rented an airfield to transport their reels to New York. Journalists representing the Black press were also there, landing in the South feeling like they had infiltrated enemy lines.

No William Faulkner was on the scene on the day the trial opened, even if the crowd mistakenly recognized him in the graying temples, mustache, and pipe of Clark Porteous, the special envoy from the *Memphis Press-Scimitar*. Similarly, people pointed or glanced meaningfully at Rob Hall, the grandson of a pastor, son of a banker, and otherwise typical Mississippian who was also a salaried employee of the *Daily Worker*, the newspaper of the American Communist Party.

Seasoned chroniclers compared this event to other great trials like those of gangster Machine Gun Kelly or the Lindbergh baby kidnapper, or, less than a year before, of Dr. Sheppard, a neurosurgeon convicted of murdering his wife. They hung out with young reporters fresh out of prestigious universities who wouldn't have missed the event for anything in the world.

THE COTTON CURTAIN

David Halberstam, the future recipient of the Pulitzer Prize and uncompromising portraitist of the "best and brightest" of the Kennedy administration, took time off to come breathe in the atmosphere. The editor in chief of the *Daily Times Leader*, the tiny Mississippi daily where he was learning the ropes, had refused to let him cover the trial.

Dan Wakefield, a young graduate of Columbia, had wangled a round-trip bus ticket from *The Nation* so he could come as a reporter. Like several of his colleagues, he was discovering the region, and his senses were being pulverized by what he saw and heard, and by having to take it all in through the sweltering air, thick with dust. "Going to the Mississippi Delta on your first trip to the South is roughly comparable to drinking a straight fifth of tequila the first time you ever try hard liquor," he later wrote.

Upon their arrival in Sumner, all these journalists had paused on the bitter irony of its publicity slogan, posted over a sign advertising Coca-Cola: "Sumner, a good place to raise a boy." This little town of under six hundred residents felt like it had been robbed of itself and, indeed, wrongly indicted. Folks would gladly have done without the largely unintended publicity caused by this trial.

Emmett Till's body had been spotted some twenty miles to the south, right where the Tallahatchie River divided two counties. If the body had been found closer to the right riverbank—part of Leflore County—instead of near the left bank, Sumner would never have been left with the trial. The town was also paying for its desire to throw some of its weight around in the region. A half century earlier, Tallahatchie County had decided to build a second courthouse. In the flood season, it was sometimes impossible to assemble in Charleston, the county seat, and those who took a chance on getting there by boat sometimes washed up dead on arrival. Sumner fought its neighbors for this courthouse without ever suspecting that this brown brick Romanesque Revival building would host one of the trials of the century.

After Emmett Till's body was discovered, Tallahatchie County Sheriff H. C. Strider took over the case from his colleagues in Leflore County, which had authority over the village of Money. Strider was weighty, both literally and figuratively. His double chin and compact two-hundred-seventy–pound frame were nothing compared to the fifteen hundred acres of cotton he grew in the region. The roof of each house occupied by his Black tenant farmers along the river had one letter of his last name painted on it. His name, S-T-R-I-D-E-R, could be seen from any of his several planes that sprayed the fields with pesticides.

Elected four years earlier, he was coming to the end of his term that year. The Mississippi Constitution prohibited him from running again. Tallahatchie County District Attorney Gerald Chatham, who was in fragile health, was serving his fourth term and had already decided to step down when it concluded at the end of the year. Both men were hoping for a quick trial and hoping to avoid passing the case onto successors.

They should have been allies but found themselves on opposing sides. The lead prosecutor was convinced that the accused were guilty. The sheriff was not defending the thesis of innocence—worse yet, he wanted to demonstrate an error or misidentification of the corpse. In his opinion, the body looked more like an adult and had decomposed too much to have been in the river for only three days. A rumor in the region was gaining momentum. People were whispering that it might be the body of a tramp who'd died of an overdose in the streets of Chicago and then been planted there to tarnish Mississippi's reputation.

❖

On September 19, a little before 10:30 a.m., Roy Bryant and J. W. Milam, the two defendants, waded through a flood of camera flashes from photographers, as they walked the few dozen yards separating the offices of their lawyers Breland & Whitten from the courthouse. It was perfectly choreographed. Bryant and Milam each had two sons. Each held the older son by the hand and carried the younger one in their arm. They were followed by their wives, both dressed in gray.

The two men had just spent three weeks in prison with only one regret in their heart: being jailed during the height of the season for picking cotton, when the farmworkers had money to spend at the grocery store and service station. Roy Bryant had been summoned for questioning on the very day of the kidnapping. J. W. Milam turned himself in the day after. The two men had acknowledged the kidnapping, but not the murder. This was their version of the story: After concluding that Emmett Till was not the boy they were looking for, they'd let him go in front of the grocery store, then they went out to play poker.

If they seemed so calm, it might have been because during the three weeks between their questioning and the trial, the current of public opinion was already turning in their favor. On the first day, Mississippians had been outraged by the murder. Leaders had called for a quick punishment to make an example of the guilty parties. Bryant and Milam could have faced a lifetime of picking cotton in the fields at the old Parchman State Penitentiary, potentially even ended up in the almost brand-new gas chamber. Inaugurated that spring, it had already served six times, but never to punish a white man convicted of murdering a Black.

But soon, a good part of the population had started taking aim at the know-it-all Yanks from the North. They rebelled when the NAACP charged that that "the state of Mississippi [had] decided to maintain white supremacy by murdering children." They didn't understand why Mamie Till had compared the state to a "den of snakes." A sinister joke soon circulated among white people that "Isn't that just like a nigger to swim across the Tallahatchie River with a gin fan around his neck."

From then on, the defendants were no longer seen as brutal hicks but as good husbands to their wives, good fathers to their sons, and good soldiers to their country. "They were never into any meanness. I raised them and I'll stand by them," their mother, Eula Lee Bryant, retorted to the press, biting her lip with emotion. This small woman with gray hair, who drank bourbon for breakfast and never went out without her .38-caliber pistol in case she ran into her runaway husband, displayed family photo albums and service records.

J. W. Milam had served as a lieutenant in Germany during World War II. He'd been hit with twenty-seven pieces of shrapnel and had the medals to prove it. And Roy Bryant, while he'd never been deployed abroad, had served as a paratrooper for three years. Thousands of dollars in donations flowed into the jars set out for that purpose next to cash registers in local stores, as well as through the mail to their lawyers. All five members of the Sumner bar association had taken on their defense.

On September 19, when they entered the courtroom, J. W. Milam and Roy Bryant were not subjected to accusatory stares by sitting on a bench facing the public, as was the case in some courtrooms. They just took a seat in a row of chairs facing the judge's platform, in front of the wooden rail that separated the public from those involved in the trial. They were surrounded by their spouses, their children, and their supporters. Behind them, the public had gathered. It felt like a good part of Mississippi was on their side.

5
THE HUNT FOR WITNESSES

Like most of the men in Sumner, Judge Curtis Swango sported a Panama hat to protect himself from the blistering sun. But it was also a tool he used at work for jury selection. On the first day of the trial, this serious judge with a reputation for equity used the hat to hold little bits of paper, each bearing the name of a potential juror, to be drawn out one by one. One hundred twenty jury candidates had been summoned this time, and twelve of them had to be retained for the trial.

It was a biased selection of the public, as it included only the names of white men. Only men because at that time, Mississippi women were denied access to serving on juries, being too commonly both placed on a pedestal and infantilized. And only white men because only registered voters could serve on a jury. And in Tallahatchie County in September 1955, not a single Black person was registered to vote.

Though a large majority of the population was Black, decades of judicial tricks had discouraged even the boldest African Americans from registering to vote. Not only did you have to pay a poll tax, you also had to be able to recopy an article of the state constitution or read it out loud and provide an interpretation that would satisfy the clerk—more or less impartial—in charge of voter registration.

For those who managed to pass that test, there remained threats of of extortion, even armed intimidation, in the workplace and in the home. Charlie Cox, the circuit clerk responsible for the voter rolls in Tallahatchie County and who was reelected to his position in early August, had promised his fellow citizens "to keep peace between the races and still continue 'OUR SOUTHERN WAY OF LIFE.'" Proclaiming this in capital letters did not indicate that the way of life included equal access to the ballot box.

For more than a day, the prosecution and the defense took turns questioning the potential jurors and releasing them if deemed necessary. Each candidate had to certify that they held no racial prejudice on the case, had never consulted with the defense lawyers, did not know the defendants personally, and had never donated a cent to their defense fund. In the end, nine of the twelve jurors retained came from the far side of the county, about thirty miles from Sumner.

Sometimes called the hill people, they were from outside the Delta region, from the foothills of the Appalachian Mountains. These were small farmers growing crops in a clay soil much less fertile than the soil of the large plantations. Their accent was different too, a little more nasal, not quite as thick.

This geographic disproportion favoring outsiders was deliberate, as each side engaged in a gamble, possibly risky, on the jury's composition. The prosecution thought it better to have jurors living as far away as possible so they'd be less likely to know the defendants J. W. Milam and Roy Bryant. The defense figured the small farmers would be less inclined to convict the two men than would the rich property owners of the Delta region, who worked with Black tenant farmers on a daily basis. The large planters were also racist, but their style was softer and more paternalistic.

So, twelve white men: nine farmers; two carpenters, including one who was retired; and one insurance agent. With one exception, they were husbands and fathers.

Their ages ranged from under thirty to over seventy. In the group photos, we see only one necktie and one dark plaid shirt among all the white shirts that are just like the shirts worn by the defendants.

The carefully selected jurors offered a good snapshot of the Southerners whom President Eisenhower had been referring to a year earlier, when he told the Supreme Court chief justice with after-dinner confidence, "These are not bad people. All they are concerned about is to see that their sweet little girls are not required to sit in school alongside some big black bucks."

On the square out in front of the courthouse, the crowd was discussing the case in two separate groups: whites on one side, Blacks on the other. The white people were waiting on the west side, with a view of the defense lawyers' offices. The Black people were gathered on the other side, at the foot of a statue erected a half century earlier to honor those defeated in the Civil War. A police officer swore to the press that none of them were locals. "Ours is out picking cotton and tending to their own business."

The Black people who'd managed to slip into the hearing room could only sit in the last two rows. The rest of the seats were reserved for whites only. Even the journalists were not allowed to mix. While the white reporters had a good view of the questioning, their Black colleagues were relegated to a small table on the right side, farther from the witness stand and the judge's podium. Sheriff Strider, who greeted them each morning with a nonchalant "Mawning, nigguhs," warned them that segregation applied to the press too.

Still, many people, both white and Black, were refused a seat. Some decided to stay and stand along the pale green plaster walls or sit on the windowsills in front of the dilapidated shades. The atmosphere was relaxed. The vast majority of the attending public took off their jackets. Beer, sandwiches, and ice cream were passed around. Presiding Judge Swango himself uncapped an ice-cold Coca-Cola during the questioning of a potential juror and allowed smoking for those who wanted to.

The reporters were amused to see the sons of the two defendants, bare to the waist, running between the rows of seats with water pistols in a game of cowboys and Indians. But behind the relaxed appearance, tension hovered in this courtroom transformed into a furnace by the late-summer humidity and the packed gallery. Two small fans turned to little effect—in any case, the tension came from farther away. During a short break, a journalist called out to J. W. Milam playfully, "Pretty hot today, huh, J. W.?"

The older defendant looked up, let the silence weigh heavy as he chewed his gum and drawled, "Enough to make a man furious."

By midmorning on Tuesday, September 20, the jury was finally complete. Everything seemed in place to start the real trial, with its parade of witnesses. Two extra attendees, more or less expected, had just arrived from the North. First, there was Mamie Till. At prosecutor Chatham's request, the mother of the deceased had agreed to come take the stand. Her friends had tried to dissuade her, fearing that she'd be risking her life in the South. The segregationist press retorted that she'd be safer in Mississippi than Chicago, the city of Al Capone.

But Mamie Till took care of her own security. She stayed in a room in Mound Bayou. A small town west of Sumner, it had been founded by freed Blacks late in the nineteenth century. She was the guest of Dr. T. R. M. Howard, the president of the Regional Council of Negro Leadership, an organization that defended the rights of Black people. This prosperous surgeon, who also owned an insurance company and a huge plantation, employed two bodyguards day and night. And in case they weren't up to the task, he kept a machine gun at the foot of his bed and a pistol on each of his bedside stands.

The second high-profile guest to appear was Charles Diggs, a Black man with a round face and intellectual eyeglasses. He was newly elected from Michigan to the House of Representatives in Washington, DC, one of only three Black men to be serving in Congress. He had family in Mississippi and knew the region well, having taken part in a rally to support voting rights for African Americans in Mound Bayou. When he arrived at the trial, the police passed around his visiting card, scratching their heads and asking, "A nigger congressman? Is that legal?" It was, and Charles Diggs took his place with the journalists of the Black press.

Whether participants or spectators at the trial, whether newly arrived or not, everyone would get an intermission more than a half-day long. Judge Swango was quite pleased to announce, in a jam-packed courtroom, a recess until the following morning. As he adjourned proceedings, the judge gave notice that starting Wednesday morning, everyone would have to be seated. If a fire had broken out in the courthouse during these first two days, the panic in the aisles would have ended in tragedy. But the security concern was separate from his decision to truncate the session. The real reason was that the prosecution had identified several extra witnesses, and some of them had not yet been located.

This dramatic, last-minute turn of events had been in the making for a couple of days, since the evening before jury selection started. Outside, behind one of the Sumner churches, a woman had delivered an anonymous scoop to James Hicks, who was a reporter for the weekly newspaper *Baltimore Afro-American*. Residents of the region had seen a Black man known as "Too Tight" with J. W. Milam and Roy Bryant on the night of the crime. To learn more about this, she whispered to Hicks, he should go to King's Place, a Black dance hall a few miles south in the village of Glendora. It was one of those grimy juke joints where after a hard day's work, plantation workers ate and got drunk, listened to blues and danced, hit on one another, or lost their shirt playing cards.

James Hicks followed the tip. At King's Place, he acted like he just happened to be there, was just passing through for a beer or two, but finally he murmured the nickname "Too Tight" to the server, like a password. The waiter pointed at a woman, and Hicks asked her to dance to gain her trust.

"Too Tight? He's in jail."

"Too Tight," whose given name was Levi Collins, was a young Black man twenty years old. He had been questioned by the police a week earlier, like the young woman's common-law husband, Henry Lee Loggins. They both worked for J. W. Milam. Hicks tried to get her to agree to the idea of visiting her partner in jail, then going out for a few drinks, but then he left. His informer had warned him that it was better not to hang around there after nightfall.

Like Mamie Till and many Black journalists, James Hicks had found a place to stay in Mound Bayou. When he went to inform T. R. M. Howard about his discoveries, he noted that the activist received corroborating information from a farmworker. The night of the murder, residents in the area had seen a group of men go past, whites and Blacks surrounding a Black teenager in the bed of a pickup truck. Later, the witnesses heard blows, followed by screams of pain and terror that grew more and more faint. They were coming from inside a barn on a farm in the village of Drew, managed by Leslie Milam, a brother of one of the defendants. When things were silent again, the pickup drove away. In the bed of the truck, they saw a tarp wrapped around something, the way they wrapped dead game to bring it home after hunting.

These revelations had the potential to change the course of the trial—or even the trial venue. If Emmett Till had been killed in Drew, the case would have to be moved to Sunflower County, west of Tallahatchie County.

To locate the two witnesses, Dr. T. R. M. Howard mobilized his network of militants, beginning with Medgar Evers, one of the most highly motivated among them. A few months earlier, the regional branch of the NAACP had recruited this insurance agent as a permanent on-the-ground activist—a field secretary. Whenever Evers sold a policy to a Black family, he took advantage of the occasion to ask them if they were on the voter rolls.

Battling segregation with the law, Medgar Evers, a veteran of Omaha Beach, had tried to pry open the racial barrier by applying to law school at the University of Mississippi. His application was, of course, rejected, despite his sarcastic assurances to the university administration. "I'm very hygienic. I bathe every day, and I assure you this brown won't rub off."

When he heard about Emmett Till's fate, Evers's tears were full of sadness, anger, and frustration. For months, he'd been flooring the accelerator of his Oldsmobile 88, crisscrossing the state to denounce racial discrimination and racist murders, and lay the groundwork for prosecutions. T. R. M. Howard asked him to swap his vehicle for an old unregistered junker while in the Delta. Evers, along with a few other activists, had just been charged with a mission to infiltrate the plantations. Dressed like farmworkers and hauling sacks of cotton on their backs, these amateur investigators had to labor in the fields, whispering questions with the hope of gaining information or catching a glance or a complicit attitude among potential informers or witnesses. It was like re-creating the Underground Railroad, except that the operation could not remain completely secret.

Once Black witnesses were identified, they would have to take the witness stand. And for that to happen, they would have to convince the prosecution of their credibility. Receptive members of the local police and the white press also had to be convinced, and were soon associated with the operation. That meant more allies, but with it a greater possibility of leaks, which was likely to frighten witnesses or put partners on alert.

The evening after the second day of the trial, these ad hoc allies had identified and located three new witnesses, but not the two extra suspects, Levi "Too Tight" Collins and Henry Lee Loggins. Those two could not be found. In the Delta, people wondered if they were hiding or in prison, as the woman at King's Place had claimed, or if they were already dead.

6
"THERE HE IS"

The evening before the trial, Mose Wright was taking a nap on his porch when some reporters stopped in to see him. In a case where the weapon, the precise time, and the location of the crime were still unknown, Mose Wright was a major witness to the abduction, and his testimony was highly anticipated.

The preacher received the journalists on his own. After the murder, his wife, Elizabeth, had purchased a one-way ticket to Chicago, hoping that he would join her there. But for the time being, Mose Wright was staying where he was. In fact, journalists who expected to find a poor, fearful man in a hovel were sorely disappointed. This old farmer earned more than most of his fellow citizens. His house was simple but tidy; he owned a refrigerator and a phonograph. A hunting rifle too. Its barrel poked out from under the bed.

Mose Wright was not flustered at the thought of testifying. He rolled out his memories of Roy Bryant's and J. W. Milam's machinations on the night of August 28 as if rehearsing for the main event. Sidney Carlton, one of the defense attorneys who had accompanied the journalists, promised them that they would hear a very different story at the trial. "Mose will tell one story in the cotton fields and quite another on the stand."

And yet, on the morning of Wednesday, September 21, the first witness called in the trial stuck to his story. In the courtroom, where those upholding the law addressed him using only his first name in a segregationist practice, Mose Wright, without faltering, once again recounted the story of the two white men bursting into his house. One of them identified himself as "Mr. Bryant." The other, he recognized as "Mr. Milam."

"Now stop a minute, Uncle Mose," interrupted Gerald Chatham, the prosecutor. "I want you to point out Mr. Milam if you see him here." The old man then rose to his feet, straightened his 5'3" frame, pointed a thin finger, and answered without hesitation and in a loud, clear voice. "There he is."

"And do you see Mr. Bryant in here?"

Without speaking, Mose Wright moved his index finger a few inches to point at the second defendant.

With this act, he was a heretic twice over: First, this Black man had identified a white man as a murderer from the witness stand. Then he did it a second time. In Mississippi, no one could remember ever having seen this. Some Black journalists had imagined such testimony and the riot that would surely follow, at which point they might have to grab a policeman's weapon to save their skin. But none of that happened. In the torrid heat of the courtroom suddenly charged with electricity, they could hear the flies buzzing.

The moment Mose Wright stood up and pointed at J. W. Milam, the camera of Black photographer Ernest Withers clicked without a flash to avoid detection by the judge. The photo, which he took as a special envoy from the *Tri-State Defender*, a weekly paper out of Memphis, showed for all posterity a man standing, head held high, eyes fixed on his target. In the foreground, the court clerk was busy taking notes on the testimonies. Shortly thereafter, a colleague who understood the value of this image paid Withers ten dollars for the roll of film.

The reverse angle of the scene, in a wide shot, comes from a white court artist sent by *Life* magazine named Franklin McMahon. The pencil sketch highlights two characters in particular. At his podium on the platform, Judge Swango is carefully observing the men Mose Wright is indicating. And at the defendants' table, the older of the two brothers, identifiable by his bald skull, is staring at the witness, his hands clasped in front of him and a closed expression on his face.

Sidney Carlton tried hard to shake up the old man for the defense during cross-examination. It was late at night, the house was not well lit, and he couldn't seriously claim to have seen the face of the two intruders through the beam of the flashlight. But Wright's message got through. At times banging his fist on the rail, at times abandoning the "sir" required of a Black witness being interrogated by a white lawyer, Mose Wright delivered a credible description of the abductors—at least of some of them, for he did not identify the third man on the porch or the person in the car who had confirmed the identity of Emmett Till. Referring to this last person, Mose Wright made only a vague observation: "It seemed like it was a lighter voice than a man's."

7
TWO MOTHERS ON THE STAND

The prosecution had scored a major victory. They seemed to have confirmed that J. W. Milam and Roy Bryant really had abducted Emmett Till. Moreover, two other witnesses, Leflore County Sheriff George Smith and his deputy John Ed Cothran, summoned to take the stand, told the court that the two men had acknowledged the abduction at the time of their arrest. But that wasn't enough for a murder conviction.

Two things still had to be proved. First, that the body found three days later in the Tallahatchie River was really that of Emmett Till. Second, that the two defendants had killed him. To resolve the first question, the prosecution called two professionals to the stand who had expertise relating to death. The first, Chester Miller, who was Black, managed a funeral parlor in Greenwood. With his own eyes, he had seen the signet ring inscribed with "L.T" down along the Tallahatchie River on the finger of a corpse that seemed to be the young man in question. The second expert, "Chick" Nelson, who was white, exercised the same profession as Miller but farther north in the town of Tutwiler, where the funerary procession had made a stop en route to Chicago. Four simple words revealed the purpose of his short testimony. Asked by the prosecutor under what name the body for which he'd been responsible had been presented, he answered, "Emmett Till."

Asked by the defense lawyer if he'd been able to determine the identity of the body independently, he answered, "No, sir."

To demonstrate what should have been evident, the prosecution kept its trump card for the end, when the victim's mother was called to the stand. Of the twenty-two witnesses who testified during the weeklong trial, Mamie was the only one who lived outside Mississippi. With her elegant black dress, her jewelry, her hat, and her fan, she represented the growing African American middle class, an image that broke with the image that whites as well as Blacks in Mississippi imagined for a Black woman.

Emmett's mother told the jury how she had examined the body meticulously, from head to foot, while it was laid out in the funeral home. "And I knew definitely that it was my boy beyond a shadow of a doubt." For purposes of identification, she was shown a photo of her son's body, taken a few hours after it was found. She took off her glasses, wiped her eyes, and buried her face in her hands. The public sat in silence. In the absence of an autopsy, who better than a mourning mother to testify to the identity of a body?

But that didn't stop J. J. Breland, the lead lawyer for the defense, from trying to insert an alternative character into the minds of the jurors, the mother as activist who would stop at nothing to advance her cause, including falsely identifying a corpse, while cashing in on life insurance along the way.

Next came the moment to confirm the assassins' identities. It was the prosecution's moment to play the three cards drawn during its recent hunt for witnesses. The most powerful was also the most fragile: Willie Reed from the village of Drew. He was a young Black man, eighteen years old. He did not have Mose Wright's strength of conviction who, in the evening of his life, had been able to turn his back on decades of submission. The frightened young man's voice was so low that Judge

Swango had to ask him to speak up several times. With little formal education, Willie Reed did not know how to gauge distance, for example, assess the difference between one hundred and five hundred yards. But that in no way diminished his devastating testimony.

On August 28, 1955, Willie Reed had gone out to run an errand at dawn when he came across a green-and-white pickup truck with four white men in the cabin and three Black men in the bed. The ones in the bed, sitting with their back to the road, were surrounding a young Black man he recognized as Emmett Till, thanks to the newspapers. A little later, he cut across the fields managed by Leslie Milam and saw the same truck parked in front of a barn. "I heard somebody hollering and I heard licks, like somebody was whipping somebody. [. . .] He was just hollering, 'Oh.'"

The young man's grandfather, Add Reed, confirmed his grandson's story. When he went out to feed the pigs, he also saw the same truck on the property. Mandy Bradley, a young woman from the neighborhood, also saw it. Willie Reed ran to her house to get help. From her kitchen window, she could see men going in and out of the barn. At one point, one of them came out to drink some water at the well, with a pistol in his belt. He was tall and balding.

While the prosecution attempted to construct a narrative of the night and fill in the blanks, the defense devised two simultaneous strategies. The first was to sow doubt on the factual elements. So, the two defendants had confessed to abducting the boy to the Leflore County sheriff and his deputy? Their lawyers attempted to invalidate these two confessions, but it was not very convincing. Police questioning had seemed more like meandering conversations than depositions, because they were speaking to local acquaintances, almost friends. This was ten years before "Miranda rights" were established, meaning police officers did not yet have to tell suspects that everything they said could be used against them.

So, Mose Wright testified that he'd recognized Roy Bryant and J. W. Milam? He'd been able to make out a bald man, vaguely, in the dark, and he'd heard another man introduce himself as Mr. Bryant, a common name. Anyway, would a criminal who had come to kidnap an adolescent be dumb enough to introduce himself using his real identity?

The defense lawyers pushed further, questioning the identity of the corpse. Not that their thesis was credible—but they had found three white witnesses, apparently qualified, to support it. There was H. D. Malone, the embalmer who had worked on the body in Tutwiler; L. B. Otken, a doctor from Greenwood; and H. C. Strider, the Tallahatchie County sheriff, "and a good one," prosecutor Chatham acknowledged.

Strider described a body so completely decomposed that the skin was falling off in strips. He could not say for sure if it was a white or a Black male. He knew the Tallahatchie River very well and estimated that the body had been underwater for at least ten days, maybe even two weeks. Ten, maybe twenty or even twenty-five days, said the embalmer, outbidding Strider. Later, it came to light that the embalmer had not actually worked on the body himself.

Dr. L. B. Otken had not performed a serious autopsy on the body but just looked at it without actually touching it. He estimated a more modest range of one to two weeks. For him, the body was so decomposed that not even the victim's brother or mother could have identified the person or his color. The prosecution counterattacked. Couldn't the body have decomposed faster if the victim was overweight and gravely wounded? "That's right."

Later, in his final statement, Gerald Chatham would take a caustic parting shot at Dr. Otken, amidst laughter.

"The taxpayers are wasting a lot of money educating a man who can't tell a white man from a negro. If Dr. Otken can't tell black from white, I don't want him to fill a prescription for me."

In parallel with this strategy of wrong suspects and the wrong corpse, the lawyers sketched out another strategy, the theory of deferred self-defense. Roy Bryant and J. W. Milam had only defended the honor of their family and Southern morals. To prove it, they called Carolyn Bryant to the stand, the woman who had allegedly suffered the offense.

The questioning started off artificially routine to establish the image of a fragile young mother. She was twenty-one years old, stood a little under 5'3", and weighed about one hundred pounds. She was married with two little boys. Upon the first question concerning the events in the grocery store on August 24, the prosecutor objected. Since no witness had established the young woman's presence at the location of the kidnapping, her experience three days prior had no relevance to the case. Judge Swango agreed. He allowed the defense to continue with the questioning and authorized the admission of a full transcript into the record, in case of appeal, but ordered the jury to leave the courtroom.

Trembling, eyes downcast, the young woman told the story of her encounter with Emmett Till. She hadn't viewed him as a Black boy afflicted with a stutter but rather as a man, "this nigger man," who spoke loudly and clearly with a Northern accent. She thought he looked taller than her by four inches and heavier by forty to fifty pounds. When she held out her hand for the money, he grabbed it and said, "How about a date, baby?" She pulled away, and he chased her, grabbed her by the waist, and said to her, "What's the matter, baby? Can't you take it?"

Lawyer Sidney Carlton approached and asked her to put his hands on her waist to illustrate what she meant. According to the young woman, Emmett Till also bragged about something, but she refused to say exactly what.

"In other words, it is an unprintable word?"

"Yes."

"Did he say anything after that one unprintable word?"

"Yes."

"And what was that?"

"Well, he said . . . well . . . 'With white women before.'"

Carolyn Bryant left the stand and took her seat next to her husband and her brother-in-law. Her testimony rang in the ears of the defense and the prosecution, the press, and the public—but not the twelve jurors. At least, not officially. For at least three weeks, the press had been reporting on the "ugly remarks" that Emmett Till had allegedly uttered to the young woman that day, and on gestures the defense kept calling an "assault." The jurors had had plenty of time to imagine the scene. And would maybe have time to have someone tell them, even though it was forbidden.

8
THE HOME OF THE BRAVE

By the morning of September 23, the parade of witnesses was coming to an end but without hearing from two who were essential: Roy Bryant and J. W. Milam.

Neither the prosecutor nor the defense lawyers wanted to put them on the stand. The prosecution worried that hearing from them would remind everyone that these were two local boys who were on trial for the murder of someone from outside the state. The defense worried that their clients might commit a blunder. Therefore, on Friday morning, the defense limited testimony to five character witnesses and disposed of them quickly. They were local elected officials, farmers, merchants, and church members who testified that J. W. Milam and Roy

THE COTTON CURTAIN

Bryant were not violent men and had good reputations. It was kind of an interlude to set up the main act: the summations and closing statements. Each side would have one hour and ten minutes to establish its vision.

The sunny early days of the trial had given way to stormy weather. The lead prosecutor, Gerald Chatham, took the floor to call for life imprisonment. He could have asked for the death penalty, but the lack of material evidence made him aim a little lower. However, that didn't prevent him from stating things with stark clarity: Shirtsleeves rolled up, occasionally mopping his face with a white handkerchief, he attacked in a deep, powerful voice. To the captive public, he sounded as much like a pastor in full sermon mode as he did a prosecutor.

He returned to the night of August 28, 1955, and the moment when Mose Wright was awakened by the sound of two men's voices out front in the dark—"Preacher!"—who had come to take his grandnephew away. "The very first word of the state's testimony was dripping with the blood of Emmett Till." For him, the crime began there, not at the grocery store. "I was born and bred in the South. I'll live and die in the South. The very worst punishment that could have occurred or should have occurred if they had any idea in their mind that this boy had done anything was to take a razor strap, turn him over a barrel, and give him a little beating."

Whether or not the body was that of Emmett Till, he considered a question settled by the testimony of his mother, the person who knew him and loved him more than anyone in the world. To illustrate his argument, Gerald Chatham told a personal story of the day when his own son had come to tell him that he'd just found his dog, Shep, who had disappeared some time before. The little boy led him to the road and pointed at the remains of a severely decomposed body. "That's ol' Shep, Pop, ol' Shep." Even though the jurors seemed extremely attentive, and Judge Swango listened carefully, sometimes holding his hands clasped in front of his face as if praying, the summation did not seem to rattle the defendants. Roy Bryant, a cigar in his mouth, put his arm around his wife's waist. J. W. Milam seemed engrossed in his newspaper.

Now it was time for the defense lawyers' summation. For fifty minutes, Chatham had worked to condemn the two defendants by employing evidence and testimonies, as well as the values of the Southern man. The lawyers for the defense of J. W. Milam and Roy Bryant spoke one by one to these same values, but adopting an apocalyptic tone. If testimony like Mose Wright's was enough to establish the two defendants' presence at the scene, argued Sidney Carlton, then any person present at this trial could find themselves wrongly accused. He knew that Carolyn Bryant's testimony probably would favor his clients' case but, knowing that the jury had not heard this testimony, he tried instead to remind them of its omission: "Where's the motive? Where's the motive?"

His colleague, J. W. Kellum, borrowed from the last lines of the national anthem to bring the jurors face-to-face with their responsibilities. "If your verdict is guilty, I want you to come to me and tell me, where is the land of the free and the home of the brave. I say to you, gentlemen, your forefathers will absolutely turn over in their graves."

The last defense lawyer to speak was John Whitten, the offspring of an influential local family. He claimed that the case had been fomented by activists ready to convince old Mose Wright to pass one body off as another by making arrangements to have it decked out with a ring. He had total confidence that the jury would hand the activists a defeat. "I'm sure every last Anglo-Saxon one of you has the courage to free these men." He said *Anglo-Saxons* as if alluding to justice and democracy in America, but everyone understood that he meant *whites*. Forty years later, Whitten would acknowledge that he'd played the race card.

It was 2:34 p.m., Friday, September 23, 1955, when Judge Swango sent the jurors into the jury room. The final words echoing in their ears had come in a concluding statement by the assistant prosecutor Robert B. Smith III. A former FBI agent, he had come to support Gerald Chatham in this difficult trial. Yes, the way of life of the South is being charged unjustly, he said. But it was exactly for that reason that the jurors must condemn the two defendants, to avoid offering magnificent propaganda to Northern activists.

The jurors hadn't been heard from since they were selected; those are the rules of the game. On Wednesday evening, an argument unrelated to the case broke out between them and a court bailiff over limits imposed on their access to media. Some of the jurors wanted to listen to the heavyweight boxing championship match between Rocky Marciano and Archie Moore on the radio. The authorities had balked, worried that the fight might highlight the issue of racial animus in the US. In the end, they were allowed to hear the white Rocky Marciano, downed briefly in the second round, win in

THE COTTON CURTAIN 75

the ninth round after delivering a knockout punch to the Black Archie Moore, who was a child of the Delta.

The jury members were also going to have to deliver a knockout decision. This would not be a win by points. The choices were either conviction or acquittal, and the decision had to be unanimous. Otherwise, they would end up with a mistrial and each side would go home without a judgment.

Filled with prejudices against Mississippi, the journalist James Hicks had revised them, despite the witnesses who vanished into the wild, by observing the strength of conviction demonstrated by the prosecution, and the balanced consideration of debates by the presiding judge. Hicks felt like he was rooting for an underdog team but one that had managed to take the lead right from the kickoff. His Southern colleagues gently mocked his hopes.

Over across the street at the *Sumner Sentinel*, expectations were increasingly feverish. The town's small weekly paper, whose office numerous journalists hung out in between hearings, normally went to press Wednesday evening. This week, it had blocked out page 1. Some of the journalists were laying bets on how long the jury deliberations would last. They would not have long to wait. A few minutes into deliberations, a juror knocked on the door to ask for Coca-Colas. Laughter rang out from inside the room, and it wasn't clear if that meant they were deriding the case or if jokes were flying around to bring down the tension.

On the first vote, nine jurors agreed on a verdict, with three still hesitant. On the second vote, only one juror remained recalcitrant. This man could block everything on his own, but he soon gave in. The third vote was unanimous. Harry Dogan, a prominent figure in the county—he had been elected sheriff during the Great Depression and was preparing to take up the post again—advised the jurors to let things drag on a little longer to make a good impression.

At 3:42 p.m., the jury filed into the courtroom that was once again lit by a hot sun. The foreman, a young local farmer, handed a yellow paper to the court clerk, who read the verdict aloud. Murmurs rose in the courtroom, which the judge interrupted with a frown. This verdict did not work for him. The twelve men would have to return to the jury room. Eight minutes later, the jury was back. Another piece of paper, another reading. This time, Curtis Swango had no objections or, if he did, he kept them to himself. It wasn't the content that had ruffled him but the lack of respect for procedure. The first time, rather than formulate their verdict in a complete sentence—"We, the jury find . . ."—as required by law, the jury had just written two simple words on the paper: "Not guilty."

SHIFTING MEMORIES (1955–2004)

9
TWO MEN FREE AND ONE HANGED

Six weeks later, J. W. Milam and Roy Bryant didn't even bother to go watch their judicial fate play out again. Even after being acquitted for the murder of Emmett Till by Tallahatchie County, the two men remained subject to the threat of an indictment—and therefore a new trial—for the abduction next door in Leflore. Normally, they should have expected such an indictment since the day of their arrest; after all, they had both acknowledged the kidnapping.

In early November 1955, Leflore County Sheriff George Smith and his deputy John Ed Cothran recounted the events to the grand jury assembled in Greenwood, a group of twenty citizens charged with examining several cases and deciding whether or not they should be brought to trial. The two primary witnesses in the Sumner trial were there as well. Mose Wright once again told the story of the kidnapping. Young Willie Reed once again said that he had seen Emmett Till on the truck being driven by the kidnappers.

The two defendants had been released at the end of September on $10,000 bail each, thanks to two local planters who paid the bonds. After that, J. W. Milam and Roy Bryant went back to work, so they were not present mid-afternoon on November 9, 1955, to see the judge pronounce before journalists the words that freed them permanently. "Gentlemen, in the case that you are interested in, there was no bill returned." The county district attorney added, "As far as I know, the case is closed."

Leflore County did not mourn the Emmett Till case; it just turned the page, with a sense of relief, even among some of the accusers. In Sumner, Deputy Sheriff Cothran had been heckled by a spectator for testifying against the defendants. The man told him with pride that the county would never condemn a white man for the murder of a Black. "That's why Tallahatchie's number one."

SHIFTING MEMORIES

Six weeks later, Cothran recognized the same man in the courthouse. The lawman had the last word: "Guess we don't indict them down here, do we? Now you tell me who's number one? Leflore's number one."

Between Roy Bryant and J. W. Milam's murder acquittal on September 23 and the dismissal of kidnapping charges on November 9, one thing had changed. America had learned a little about Emmett Till. Not about him directly, or what he had done or not done in the grocery store, but about his father, Louis Till, the man who had left him the signet ring bearing his initials from beyond the grave. This was the ring that had contributed to the identification of the adolescent's body.

At the trial, the name Louis Till was hardly mentioned. During Mamie Till's testimony, the prosecution asked her only if Emmett's father was still alive.

"No, sir. He died in the service."

"He died in service?"

"Yes, sir."

"Do you remember the date of his death?"

"Yes, sir; the second of July, 1945."

"Where was he when he died?"

"In the European Theatre."

That's all that was needed for *Life* magazine, one of America's most read weeklies, to rise up after J. W. Milam and Roy Bryant's acquittal. The murder of a young Black boy was going unpunished, even though he was the son of a soldier killed in Europe, "fighting for the American principle that all men are equal."

When he read these lines at his home in Alabama, reporter William Bradford Huie was puzzled. A former war correspondent known for bestsellers that were appreciated by Hollywood, he knew that Black Americans had represented a tiny part of those who had died at the front in World War II. Because they were relegated by segregation to the rear lines, they were most often cooks, drivers, or workers for the white units. However, there was one category where they constituted the majority of deaths, but it was hidden from public view like a shameful secret, and that was soldiers condemned to death for crimes committed in uniform, most often rape or murder, and sometimes both.

For two years, the journalist had kept a list of these executions in his desk drawer. He had not forgotten his journey to the Picardy countryside in late 1953, while writing his book titled *The Execution of Private Slovik*. That sunny autumn afternoon, the fields seemed to be literally nourished with blood. Not red from the beetroots, but real blood. The blood of fallen soldiers in the First World War, and then the Second.

Huie had an appointment with both wars at his destination, the Oise-Aisne American Cemetery. Over six thousand American soldiers who had fallen in the region during the Great War in 1918 were buried there on four parcels of land. Among them were several hundred unidentified soldiers, "KNOWN BUT TO GOD," said their gravestones. But what had intrigued Huie were the other anonymous graves. Set apart on the other side of the two-lane road, hidden behind an administrative building of white stone with a tile roof, and closed to public access, was a fifth parcel containing the graves of Americans executed in Europe and North Africa during World War II. There were four rows of graves, ninety-six in total, behind a single white cross. A small plaque bearing only a number was all that identified the occupants of the graves for the administration.

William Bradford Huie had been interested in the soldier in tomb No. 65, Eddie Slovik. In late January

1945, he was the first soldier to be executed for desertion since the Civil War. He had been put to death by firing squad in Alsace. To obtain permission to visit his grave, Huie had to negotiate with a colonel at the Pentagon. When the colonel left the office for a moment, Huie seized the opportunity to copy down most of the list of names corresponding to the graves, thinking it might be useful at some point. And he was right: In the lower left-hand corner of the parcel, grave No. 73, was that of a certain Louis Till.

William Bradford Huie's hunch was quickly confirmed. On October 14, 1955, the *Jackson Daily News* broke the story on page 1 that Louis Till, the man who had given the teenager killed in the Delta his middle name, had not died of war wounds as a hero. The Till family and those who had supported them had lied, at least by omission. In the summer of 1945, Mamie Till had received a death certificate listing "deliberate misconduct" as the cause of death. The information had been served up to the *Jackson Daily News* by Mississippi Senator James Eastland, a "Dixiecrat," one of the Southern Democrats fiercely opposed to desegregation. When contacted by the newspaper, he tapped his sources in the military and obtained Louis Till's military record.

The file revealed that Emmett Till's father, along with a comrade in the same company, had been convicted of killing a woman, Anna Zanchi, and raping two other women named Frieda Mari and Benni Lucretzia on June 27, 1944, a night of chaos provoked by an antiaircraft barrage near Rome. Both men had been condemned to death. Much later, members of their regiment would share certain doubts. Louis Till had never admitted guilt. Other soldiers had confessed their guilt in this case in exchange for immunity or in the hope of a less severe punishment. Furthermore, the victims had not identified their assailants. It didn't matter; General Eisenhower's second-in-charge on the European front had approved the order for execution.

During his final days, "St. Louis Till," as his comrades called him, probably because he'd been born in Missouri, had shared the same cellblock as the fascist poet Ezra Pound at a camp near Pisa. The writer, jailed for treason, had begun to compose his *Pisan Cantos* on a tablet in pencil. On July 3, 1945, he scribbled these words: "Till was hung yesterday/for murder and rape with trimmings."

Emmett Till had barely known his father, who had gone off to war when Emmett was a year old and had only come home on leaves that sometimes seemed more like desertion. But for the Mississippi segregationists, Emmett now shared some of his father's faults. As the saying goes, "Like father, like son." So, for part of America, the murderers of Emmett Till had not punished a young jokester—more likely, they had killed off a budding criminal.

10
CONFESSIONS FOR SALE

The drawing, which took up half a page, seemed to have come straight out of a nineteenth-century popular novel. It showed two men who looked like bad guys and their victim. One of them, with a receding hairline, was holding a pistol. The one with a dark crew cut looked just as fierce as his buddy. At their feet was a naked teenager on his knees, his bowed head next to a fan leaning against a branch. In the background, a menacing forest loomed. The title on the left-hand page hooked the reader: "The Shocking Story of Approved Killing in Mississippi."

The article appeared in *Look* magazine on January 10, 1956. *Look* was a biweekly family magazine brimming with ads. The magazine had advertised this issue in the big daily newspapers, which promised never-before-printed, never-before-read information on the Emmett Till case—for good reason. The author, William Bradford Huie, was publishing the confessions of J. W. Milam and Roy Bryant, the two murderers.

Huie had paid them for their story but did not make this clear to readers.

After digging into the memories of the little cemetery in Picardy, the Alabama journalist could have scooped his fellow reporters on Louis Till but said he hadn't wanted to. He didn't want people believing that Emmett Till was responsible for the acts of his father. However, William Bradford Huie was not finished with the case. He was not motivated by political engagement, even though this pure Southerner had been raised by a father who'd fought the Ku Klux Klan, and believed in the progress of civil rights.

What Huie believed in most of all was a good story. He was fascinated by cases where sexual taboos intersected with murderous rage. As a young reporter twenty years earlier, one particular trial had made an impression on him. It was the trial of a young Black man accused of raping a white woman in his home state of Alabama. When the defendant denied the charges, Huie had seen the woman's husband pull out a gun right there in the courtroom during the trial and the jury issue the death penalty in only five minutes. Huie had even gone to the state prison to witness the execution, one of those nights when "the state fries black meat and sometimes white meat," and claimed to have held the tormented man's hand a few moments before his body convulsed with the jolt of 2,300 volts of electricity.

Huie was convinced of the novelistic character of the Till case but didn't see it in the newspaper accounts of the trial of J. W. Milam and Roy Bryant. All he could see was a battle of hypocritical arguments that clarified neither the personality nor the acts of the defendants or the victim. It was frustrating. He was sure that for a price, it would be possible to publish the truth.

William Bradford Huie had not invented "checkbook journalism"; he'd been just an infant when the *New York Times* paid a telegrapher on the *Titanic* $1,000 for his story of the shipwreck. Anyway, Huie was prepared to justify it openly. If paying a few thousand dollars was what it would take to get to the truth, the price was worth it. After all, the FBI was doing the same thing with informants. The theory held even better for cases involving Southern racist murders; most of the good sources were guilty or complicit. Might as well grill them instead of just recopying the story provided by the investigation that had been conducted by the authorities, which was necessarily unfinished and incomplete.

As a point of entry into the case, he chose J. J. Breland and John Whitten, two of the lawyers charged with defending J. W. Milam and Roy Bryant. These well-known figures in the Delta, who were employed on an ongoing basis by the local banks and plantations, would understand the need to shed light on the crime for the good of the community. Like them, William Bradford Huie was a Southerner of long lineage and maybe even belonged to the same fraternity.

Upon his arrival in Sumner, he questioned John Whitten, diving in headfirst. Did the lawyer agree with him that the two defendants were guilty and had killed this boy at the conclusion of a drunken revenge expedition gone bad? The lawyer retorted that he hadn't even asked the question because he didn't want to know the answer and especially didn't want to have to tell his wife.

His associate J. J. Breland hammered his point that "there ain't gonna be no nigger votin'. If any more pressure is put on us, Tallahatchie River won't hold all the niggers that'll be thrown into it." His remarks regarding

SHIFTING MEMORIES

the defendants were just as sharp and crude. His opinion was, for Emmett Till, they should have just imposed a thirty-and-nine, the ancient punishment of thirty-nine lashes with the whip that had been applied to recalcitrant slaves. But, he supposed, they probably let their own brutality get the best of them and Milam had decided to finish the job. "Milam comes from a big, mean, overbearing family. Got a chip on his shoulder. That's how he got that battlefield promotion in Europe; he likes to kill folks. [But] hell, we've got to have our Milams to fight our wars and keep the niggahs in line."

The lawyers and their clients accepted William Bradford Huie's monetary proposition. The two acquitted defendants would share a little over $3,000, which meant, for each, enough revenue to support a family in that area for a year or two. The lawyers would receive about $1,000. In exchange, J. W. Milam and Roy Bryant would agree to release their story and adaptation rights, and they would agree not to sue for defamation.

For two evenings in mid-October 1955, starting at nightfall, the law office library echoed with their account of Emmett Till's murder. J. W. Milam spoke more, with his younger partner intervening mostly on the incident at the grocery store.

A few days later, Roy Bryant brought Carolyn along for the contract signing, where she caught the eye of William Bradford Huie. The journalist had asked his editor in chief to send him a lawyer who could drink bourbon from the bottle without blanching: "Let's don't send a preacher to the whorehouse." Turned out that the New York jurist who had driven in from the Memphis Airport with a bag full of cash was terrified by his first visit to the South, but that didn't prevent the formalities from proceeding without a hitch. After the documents had been signed, the Northerner and one of the murderers even found a common interest in military firearms. J. W. Milam had come with his Colt .45, the gun which he claimed to have used to kill Emmett Till with a shot in the temple.

William Bradford Huie waited for the case in Leflore County to be dismissed before publishing his article. Now acquitted of the murder of Emmett Till in Tallahatchie County, J. W. Milam and Roy Bryant could no longer be tried for that crime by the state of Mississippi, even if they confessed. And with Leflore County declining to charge them with kidnapping, the two men seemed to be in the clear, judicially speaking. Thus, there was no reason not to publish the testimony of the two half brothers, for whom the "half" was just a legal formality. In practical terms, they were both part of a "lusty and devoted" clan where they "work, fight, vote, and play as a family," wrote Huie. And where they also killed as a family.

After the abduction, the two men said in the article, they had driven west for a while with the idea of making the teenager learn a lesson by standing him at the edge of a sheer cliff, one hundred feet above the river. But because they were unable to find that spot, they turned back to J. W. Milam's house in the village of Glendora. There, they said they pistol-whipped Emmett Till in a barn for quite a while, just like J. W. had beaten German prisoners under his guard during the war. The two men had been exasperated by the combative attitude of their captive. "You bastards, I'm not afraid of you. I'm as good as you are. I've 'had' white women. My grandmother was a white woman." At that point, J. W. Milam declared him a dead man.

According to William Bradford Huie's article, during the interview, Milam paused his description of the night to launch into a segregationist tirade. "As long as I live and can do anything about it, niggers are gonna stay in their place. Niggers ain't gonna vote where I live. If they did, they'd control the government. They ain't gonna go to school with my kids. And when a nigger gets close to mentioning sex with a white woman, he's tired o' livin'."

After the beating in the barn, the two men and their prisoner set out again, this time heading for Boyle, a village about thirty miles away, where a new cotton gin had just been installed. They'd made Emmett load the old fan into the truck, then come back to Glendora, just as the sun was rising over the village and the banks of the Tallahatchie River. There, Milam had ordered the teenager to strip down completely, then interrogated him one last time.

"You still as good as I am?"

"Yeah."

"You still 'had' white women?"

"Yeah."

At this, the older half brother shot the victim dead, then wired the fan around his neck for ballast. Together, Bryant and Milam dumped Emmett's body into the muddy waters of the Tallahatchie River. Back at J. W. Milam's house, the two men lit a fire in the yard to destroy Emmett Till's clothes and shoes, the last traces of the murder.

❖

SHIFTING MEMORIES

When negotiating with Bryant and Milam after their acquittal, William Bradford Huie had warned them he would be scouring the region to corroborate their statements. At the smallest lie, he would tear up the contract. His narrative of the murder was, by definition, closer to the truth than the acquittal pronounced in Sumner, yet still manipulative.

At the trial, Mose Wright's testimony had implied possible involvement of Carolyn Bryant in the kidnapping. In contrast, William Bradford Huie asserted that the two murderers had been informed of the grocery store incident by a Black resident in the area and that they had not presented Emmett to their spouse and sister-in-law Carolyn. Huie was convinced that Carolyn Bryant bore no responsibility, his strongest argument being that she could have told her brother-in-law, J. W. Milam, about the incident as early as August 24, when he'd stopped in at the grocery store that evening. Furthermore, Huie didn't even mention the barn in Drew where Emmett was tortured, or the existence of possible accomplices, though he'd seemed convinced of it at the start. Accomplices who, it must be said, could still have been charged with murder.

The work of the Alabama journalist had all the hallmarks of a romanticized narrative and a snow job, for the *Look* magazine readers who would believe that these two men—and only these two—were responsible for Emmett Till's death. For the defenders of the victim's memory, as well. At first, Huie, an expert in double-dealing, tried to get the NAACP to finance his reporting by promising them to turn it into a book that would be "more explosive than *Uncle Tom's Cabin*—and a lot more honest." He was referring to the novel by Harriet Beecher Stowe that had been instrumental in shifting attitudes on slavery. But the NAACP didn't bite and, in the end, Emmett Till's family and the Black activists had to accept a bitter victory. The two men who'd been acquitted had clearly confessed, however, the article had also presented their victim as totally unaware of the danger and almost suicidal, and it perpetuated the defense's account of the incident at the grocery store.

J. W. Milam and Roy Bryant had also been duped, and William Bradford Huie had felt it coming. When Bryant had finally consented to the article after long hesitation, the journalist remarked to his editor in chief with irony, "The poor bastard! [. . .] He has already lost his business, and most of those people who 'approve' of what he has done will now find ways to avoid him. Three months from now, the folks who put up the money for his defense won't speak to him on the street."

Indeed, when Huie returned to the area in early 1957, he noticed that although locals in the area had defended the two accused men at the height of the case, they had dropped them since. Boycotted by the Black clientele, both men had been forced to sell their stores. Bryant, after a vain attempt to get a job with the police force, had gone back to being a welder, thanks to a veteran's assistance program. Milam had only been able to get a bank loan to develop his crops with help from his lawyer.

Taking long pulls on a cigarette in his pickup truck, he delivered his lessons learned regarding the case. "You can do sumpin' that everybody says you oughta done. Like killin' a German . . . or killin' a niggah who gets outta place. Everybody slaps you on the back for it. Hell, they give you a medal! Then . . . after a while . . . those same folks won't come around you . . . they won't even like you . . . because you done it."

In any case, most people didn't question who the murderers were. In fall 1956, a few months after the *Look* article, Tallahatchie County published annual crime figures. Four homicides had been committed in the county in the previous year and the form listed four victims, including Emmett Till. Even though no one had been convicted of his murder, the local sheriff was clear. Two names were listed next to his name with the mention "the following persons committed the homicides listed": J. W. Milam and Roy Bryant.

11
THE DREAM AND ITS MARTYRS

The final product was a two-hundred–page typed document brimming with footnotes and assembled under a solemn title: "A Case Study of Southern Justice." In Tallahassee, August 1963, Hugh Stephen Whitaker defended his master's thesis at Florida State University, a study devoted to the Emmett Till case.

Whitaker, a member of the Pi Sigma Alpha political science honor society, was approaching his twenty-fourth birthday. In photos of the time, he looks composed, with hair parted on the side and large white teeth. However, he was more daring than he looked. A native of Charleston, the Tallahatchie County seat, this student wanted to shed light on the crime that had marked his teenage years.

To conduct research commensurate with his ambition, he needed to consult the archives at the other university in Florida's capital, the university for Black students. Thanks to a sympathetic librarian, Whitaker went over there, sometimes at nightfall, entering through a back door to dig into the old copies of African American newspapers, which were rich in information relating to the Emmett Till case that had been overlooked by other sources. One night, when there were riots in Tallahassee, members of the football team provided protection to assure that he'd get off campus safely.

When Whitaker conducted an on-the-ground investigation in Mississippi during the summer of 1962, the situation was even more heated. James Meredith's demand to be admitted to "Ole Miss," the venerable state university just outside the Delta region, had electrified the local white supremacists. In fact, just a few weeks after his departure, a riot would leave two dead on campus. It was not the best time to be stirring the embers of the Emmett Till affair. There were days when Whitaker found threatening anonymous notes on the windshield of his Volkswagen.

Fortunately, in addition to being from the Delta region himself, he knew someone who would open doors for him. His mother's second husband was one of Sheriff Strider's former deputies. The two men shared memories and sources. Whitaker had also dreamed of questioning William Faulkner, Mississippi's most famous son, but Faulkner died of a heart attack shortly after falling off a horse a few days before Whitaker started his investigations. Other than that, it was happy hunting.

James Hamilton Caldwell, the third lawyer in the prosecution team during the 1955 Sumner trial, admitted that the trial proceedings of J. W. Milam and Roy Bryant had been for show. "The case was lost from the start. A jury would turn loose any man who killed a Negro over insulting a white woman."

On the other side, one of the richest sources turned out to be J. J. Breland. Over a nice bottle of Jack Daniel's, the lead defense lawyer opened up and delivered secrets of the trial. Having been tipped off by the future county sheriff, he knew the jurors' profiles and had been able to make sure that they were safe bets. After that, he confided, any student in first-year law school would have won. He was also open about another important bit of information. The prosecution, the press, and civil rights activists had all been unable to put their hands on Henry Lee Loggins and Levi "Too Tight" Collins, the murderers' possible Black accomplices, because Sheriff

Strider had put them in prison in Charleston under false names.

Whitaker also heard in the Delta that during the trial, the local branch of the Citizens' Councils, an organization of prominent local supremacists, had allegedly contacted the jurors to recommend that they vote "the right way." The jurors Whitaker was able to question by promising them anonymity admitted that they had not swallowed the tale of the mistaken corpse and believed that J. W. Milam and Roy Bryant were guilty. Of course, they had claimed the opposite to the press when they delivered the verdict, but time had passed since then, and Milam and Bryant had confessed.

Whitaker could not help noting evidence of judicial error. He wrote about it, but it was as if his investigation didn't exist. As soon as he defended his thesis, it went to gather dust on a shelf in the library, like so many others, and he immediately shifted his energies to a different project, a doctoral thesis on the consequences of Black voters' enfranchisement in Mississippi. Of course, he would have liked to pull an article or a book out of his work, but he feared reprisals against his family, who still lived in Mississippi. Financial reprisals or worse.

That same 1963 summer, when Hugh Stephen Whitaker was defending his master's thesis, August 28 marked eight years since J. W. Milam and Roy Bryant had abducted and killed Emmett Till. That was plenty of time to upend the fate of several protagonists in the affair. After his sensational deposition in Sumner, Great-Uncle Mose Wright had slept in his car for several nights, as people had noted suspect comings and goings at his house. Soon thereafter, the man who had planned to die in Mississippi, where he'd been born, fled to Chicago, leaving behind part of his cotton harvest and his dog Dallas. He went with a heavy heart and with a dream. "I'm gonna keep praying for the day when there's a hollering, 'Preacher, Preacher,' outside my door. And when I look out, I want to see someone on his knees begging forgiveness for killing my boy."

Emotionally exhausted, the trial witness Willie Reed also fled to Chicago. He made himself keep his mouth shut and forget what he had lived through. Dr. T. R. M. Howard, put on a kill list by the local supremacists, chose to pack his bag and head in the same direction rather than end up in a coffin. As for Gerald Chatham, the prosecutor who had experienced terrible pressure for leading the prosecution, he died of a heart attack on October 9, 1956, only a few months after celebrating his fiftieth birthday.

The killers had also almost disappeared from the landscape. Since giving their confessions to the press, J. W. Milam and Roy Bryant sometimes received threatening letters or phone calls, especially in August. But more often, it was as if they didn't exist. Their country seemed to want to forget them. After selling his store and retraining as a welder, Roy Bryant left, moving his family to a naval construction yard in southern Louisiana for a short time, then found work in a steel factory in eastern Texas. In summer 1961, while sitting at a traffic light, Bryant noticed that the vehicle next him had Tallahatchie County license plates, so he greeted the driver, saying, "I'm Roy Bryant." The other man's smile faded and he took off without a word.

Roy's half brother also came to live in Texas after feeling the mute disavowal of his fellow Delta residents more than once. One incident in particular stood out. One day in 1960, J. W. Milam, who had long been known to traffic bootleg whiskey, retrieved an illegal still in the hills and displayed it in broad daylight in the streets of Charleston. One of the jurors from the Emmett Till trial felt like he'd been had. "To think of all we did for him, and he goes and does something like that."

America was moving forward without them. On August 28, 1963, a certain America marched on Washington in a great demonstration in support for civil rights. For that part of the country, the Emmett Till case was not a bad memory to be pushed aside but rather a symbol—even a detonator.

Sunday, November 27, 1955. The case had been over for less than three weeks when T. R. M. Howard, the activist doctor from Mound Bayou who had lodged Mamie Till during the trial, gave a speech on the case in the Baptist church on Dexter Avenue in Montgomery, Alabama. His host was the young pastor of the church who had arrived there the previous year, a certain Martin Luther King Jr.

At the time, like Mamie Till, Howard then drew crowds all over the country. From church hall to banquet hall, he warned in his clear, vibrant, outraged voice about the terror that was striking Mississippi. In the unpunished murder of Emmett Till, he saw a rallying moment for the Blacks of the South, and maybe for the whole country. They were not safe from violence even in their homes. In his speeches, he called out J. Edgar Hoover, the unremovable head of the FBI. How was it possible that the agency had been able to unmask a man who had exploded a plane with dynamite above Colorado in less than two weeks, yet seemed incapable of dealing with the murder of Black people in the South?

Sitting on one of the filled pews on Dexter Avenue, a seamstress named Rosa Parks had come almost as a neighbor. She worked just five hundred yards away, across the street at the Montgomery Fair department store. As a Methodist, she'd had little chance to spend time in this red-brick church, located just across from the state capitol building, but for ten years, she'd been an NAACP activist. Like many, she'd been moved to tears by the photos of Emmett Till's corpse. In fifty years, after her death, a letter from that time would be found in her drawer, a letter written in pencil on her employer's letterhead to an unknown or imaginary correspondent. In it, she described the daily lived experience of segregation, with separate bus seats, restaurant counters, drinking fountains, *Whites Only* to one side, *Colored* to the other. In slanted script, near the end, she mentioned the lynching of Emmett

Till—but she also had others who were less well known on her mind.

At what moment does a case, not at all isolated, stop being *just one more* and become *one too many*, setting off, consciously or not, a move toward action? Dates coincide at moments when history accelerates. Four days after Dr. Howard's visit to Alabama, Rosa Parks refused to give up her seat on the bus to a white passenger and ended up at the police station. Four days after that, on December 4, 1955, Martin Luther King Jr. called his fellow citizens to action. Exactly one hundred days after the death of Emmett Till, the Montgomery bus boycott, a foundational moment in the civil rights movement, officially began.

By 1963, Martin Luther King Jr. had grown famous. Rosa Parks had too, even though apparently not enough for her to be given time to pronounce more than a dozen words or so at the very masculine rostrum during the march on Washington. "Hello, friends of freedom. It's a wonderful day . . ."

On this August 28, however, Mamie Till wasn't even there in the capital. Like her son's murderers, Mamie

Till had soon returned to anonymity. She'd gone back to school and married her beau, Gene Mobley, with Emmett's joke in the back of her mind, the comment he'd made before setting off to Mississippi: "Don't you and GeGe run off and get married before I get back." Sitting in front of her television on this anniversary of her son's kidnapping, she had the curious feeling of being left on the sidelines, while also being part of something immense by proxy. In truth, she should have been in Washington. The organizers had invited her, but her own mother, alarmed about her safety, had hidden the invitation.

Her mother wasn't the only one who worried. To avoid having hundreds of thousands of African Americans leaving the federal capital at nightfall, the organization had imposed a time limit on the speakers. It applied to Martin Luther King as well as the others. People close to him had encouraged him to cut a recurring passage from his recent speeches to avoid wearing out the audience. It was the passage where he described his dreams for the future. But that advice didn't take into account the solemnity of the moment or the crowd's fervor or gospel singer Mahalia Jackson's heartfelt cry in the middle of his speech. "Tell them about the dream, Martin! Please, tell them about the dream!" So, he did. *"I have a dream."*

Sitting in front of her small television screen, Mamie Till was captivated as she heard Martin Luther King's dream that one day, even Mississippi would be transformed into an "oasis of freedom and justice." She didn't know that several weeks earlier, in Detroit, the pastor had expressed a more precise dream in his speech. "I have a dream that there will be a day that we will no longer face the atrocities that Emmett Till had to face or Medgar Evers had to face, that all men can live with dignity."

Medgar Evers, the activist who had tracked down the witnesses for the Emmett Till murder trial, had himself been assassinated on June 12, 1963, in Jackson, the capital of Mississippi. He was shot in the back as he got out of his car by a killer concealed in a honeysuckle thicket, armed with a telescopic rifle. He bled to death in front of his wife and children.

The name Emmett Till was also beginning to circulate in popular culture. In March 1962, Bob Dylan, who was getting ready to record his first album, was playing his new title, "The Death of Emmett Till," for the first time. In the ballad, the narrator says that he's read about the case in the papers but can't tolerate seeing "the smiling brothers walkin' down the courthouse stairs." The song didn't stick to historical truth, implying that the two murderers had confessed to their crime during the trial and that some of their accomplices were sitting in the jury. Emmett Till, Roy Bryant, and J. W. Milam, as flesh-and-blood beings, disappeared behind their status as icons of scorned childhood and shameless impunity.

Bob Dylan would soon stop playing "The Death of Emmett Till," but the following year, in the summer of 1963, another singer tried again with more success, penning a song about a boy in Mississippi who "got a taste of Southern law." Half folk balladeer, half reporter, Phil Ochs included these lyrics in his song "Too Many Martyrs." Ochs was so afraid of being shot during his concerts in the South that he asked other musicians to scan the audience to look for armed spectators.

After Emmett Till, the number of martyrs kept climbing, especially in Mississippi, where the violence and terror stood out even among Southern states. Whether or not they were activists, African Americans were being beaten, tortured, shot, and drowned.

One case in particular left a deep impression on America. The three victims were James Chaney, a young African American man from eastern Mississippi, and Andrew Goodman and Michael Schwerner, two young Jewish men from New York. They were all participating in "Freedom Summer," a mobilizing effort to support Black voter registration in the state.

On June 21, 1964, the three young activists disappeared while driving together late at night near Philadelphia, Mississippi, about sixty miles from where Emmett Till had been killed. An anguished search took place before television cameras and lasted forty long days. Just like nine years earlier, elected officials suggested that they had faked their disappearance, claiming that the three men had fled to Cuba. Just like nine years earlier, America had, in the end, learned that in Mississippi, they don't kidnap, they kill. Murdered in cold blood by white supremacists who'd been tipped off by the local police, the three men were finally found, buried in the red clay of a dam.

On August 7, 1964, a young Black activist named Dave Dennis mounted the rostrum to pronounce James Chaney's eulogy. His head bobbed with pain, and his nasal voice was constantly close to breaking. "I can remember the Emmett Till case, what happened to him, and what happened to the people who killed him. They're walking the streets right now and the brother of one is a police officer in a place called Ruleville, Mississippi."

The activist did not mention J. W. Milam and Roy Bryant by name, but he knew their family tree. That brother was known for harassing civil rights activists at their homes and in the middle of the night. Half collapsing on the podium, the young militant could feel that this case in Philadelphia would end like the case of Emmett Till. "When they find the people who killed these guys in Neshoba County, you've got to come back to the state of Mississippi and have a jury of their cousins, their aunts, and their uncles. And I know what they're going to say—not guilty. Because no one saw them pull the trigger." While murmurs of disapproval rose from the audience, he continued, "I'm tired of that! See, another thing that makes me even tireder, though, that is the fact that we as people here in the state and the country are allowing this to continue to happen, even us as black folk."

12
"IF I DID IT"

Mamie Till had a question for one of her son's two killers. The only one surviving, for it had been five years since J. W. Milam had died of cancer at the age of sixty-one on Saint Sylvester's Day, December 31, 1980. Dressed in a black-and-purple striped dress, her features filled out and accentuated by her large round glasses, Emmett Till's mother made a reappearance before the cameras. Calmly, she addressed a message to Roy Bryant. "I would like to know what life has been like for him. I don't feel that I have wallowed in the grief of my son's death. I feel that I have moved on from there, and I've gone on to do things that were profitable, that I've reached out and I've helped other people. But I just wonder how Mr. Bryant's life has been. I almost feel sorry for him."

Rich Samuels, the journalist across from her, had met her by chance on November 21, 1984, during a rally in memory of another—yet another—teenager found dead. This one, named Ben Wilson, was seventeen years old. A rising star in basketball, he'd been cut down by two bullets during a confrontation with two boys of his own age as he came out of his high school in Chicago.

Rich Samuels, a reporter for WMAQ-TV, a local NBC affiliate, only vaguely remembered Emmett Till. The Black Chicago residents that Samuels stopped on the sidewalk to interview remembered him even less. "Emmett Till? I never heard of him." Mamie told him everything. From then on, Samuels was determined to work his way back through time, which explains why he started working on production of a documentary titled *The Murder and the Movement*.

At a barbershop, he asked two witnesses to talk about the abduction. Wheeler Parker and Simeon Wright, Emmett's two cousins, had stayed out of the spotlight for three decades. He took advantage of the fact that famous figures such as Medgar Evers's widow and the writer James Baldwin came to Chicago to ask them their memories of the case. Baldwin had authored a play titled *Blues for Mister Charlie*, inspired by the murder of Emmett Till.

SHIFTING MEMORIES

He spent hours in a South Side library reading old news reports and came across the photo of the corpse of Emmett Till published by *Jet* magazine. Black America had seen it at the time, and it was now time to show it to white America. But would Roy Bryant agree to talk about the case again? Divorced from Carolyn and remarried, he now owned a different grocery store in a Black neighborhood in Ruleville, about thirty miles west of Money. The best way to find the boss when he wasn't expecting you was to stop in at the store on Saturday when everybody was spending the money they'd earned during the week.

The gamble worked, but with no payoff. Roy Bryant was in the store; however, he did not want to speak. Brandishing a bottle like a club, he threatened to take a swing at the film technician. When the documentary came out, it showed a thick man, open shirt showing suspenders, and a cigarette hanging from his lip, pointing a threatening finger at the camera.

In 1985, Rich Samuels wasn't the only one working hard to put the name Emmett Till back on page 1. For the past few years, fellow journalists had conducted dozens of interviews for a documentary series on the struggle for civil rights, a project named *Eyes on the Prize* that promised to have immense success. Journalists at Blackside production company realized that all the activists they interviewed had been devastated by the fate of the teenager from Chicago. It suited their purpose: They'd already planned to have the Emmett Till murder open the first episode of the series. In short, they would make it the original scene of the civil rights movement.

They even made a trip to Money in the late 1970s to film at Bryant's former grocery store—until local residents showed up with rifles to chase away the "nigger movie crew." They also dreamed of interviewing Roy Bryant and J. W. Milam, maybe to extract real confessions from them, on film and not paid. But the two men could not be found.

Press journalist Joe Atkins had better luck than his colleagues in television. In summer 1985, his employer, the *Clarion-Ledger*, Mississippi's largest daily newspaper, was looking at the big picture. Usually, the anniversary of Emmett Till's murder went unremarked, but this year, the thirtieth anniversary, they'd give it several pages of coverage, including on page 1.

The journalist was assigned the mission of obtaining an interview with Roy Bryant at his grocery store, a former gas station, with a back room outfitted as a small café with three red booths, a bar, and a pool table. When Atkins arrived, a cat was napping on a pile of grocery bags. The reporter noticed a video cassette of a recent episode of the NBC *Today Show*, which had shown excerpts from *The Murder and the Movement*.

Roy Bryant, the young, athletic man who had been compared to Marlon Brando during coverage of the 1955 trial, had now lost his hair and his arrogance. Because his years as a welder in Louisiana and Texas had left him almost blind, he needed a magnifying glass to read the prices on the products in the aisles. The preceding year, he had copped a fine and probation for fraud relating to food stamps. Turns out he was buying them at half their value from consumers who needed cash and then turning them in to the government for full reimbursement.

He agreed to chat with a friend at his side as a body-guard, but he wouldn't go into the substance of the Emmett Till case—especially not for free, claiming that he'd never seen a dime of the money promised for the *Look* article. The Emmett Till case, he affirmed, was like Emmett himself, dead and thirty years buried. And had to stay like that. Anyway, nobody could do anything to him. "Hell no, I didn't do it! I didn't admit it then. You don't expect me to admit it now. Of course, they couldn't do anything to me if I did."

It was as if he was now the commentator on a case that had made him famous and which he didn't want to be associated with him. "I feel this way: If Emmett Till hadn't got out of line, it probably wouldn't have happened to him." Hearing these words, Joe Atkins, who hadn't pulled out his Dictaphone to avoid scaring off the interviewee, stopped taking notes and engraved this quote as he waited for the rest. Which didn't come. That was as close as Roy Bryant would get to the truth, at least his truth.

Then, nine years later, it started again. Someone knocked on his door. On February 7, 1994, it was his second wife who opened it. Before her stood a man who introduced himself as Plater Robinson. "Hello! How are you! Is Mr. Bryant here?"

Lying on the sofa in front of a country music show on television, Roy Bryant got to his feet with difficulty. He had cancer and was suffering intense pain in his back. Things were not going well. He'd spent eight months in prison in 1988 after going back to trafficking food stamps. His grocery store had burned down, so he was now living off the modest profits of a fireworks store, selling watermelons out of the back of his truck, and renting slum properties to African Americans. Broke, he'd gone to see his former lawyer, John Whitten, to ask for help. But all Whitten could advise was to sell his story again—that is, if he could find someone to buy it.

At first, Roy Bryant was talkative with this unknown visitor. But his tone changed when he learned the man's profession. Plater Robinson worked at the radio station of *Christian Science Monitor*, a daily newspaper with a good reputation. He'd come to ask him about the Emmett Till case, of course. A decade after returning to the glare of the media, the acquitted murderer stuck to his line. It was time to let this case die.

"A lot of people made a damn bunch of money out of it. I ain't never made a damn nickel," he spit in his thick, drawling voice. But mixed with these usual feelings—irritation, bitterness, anger—there was a new note of fear. "Look what they're doing to Beckwith down there now, [. . .] and now they want to get me! So, hell with 'em. I'm not trying to be ugly, but I just won't talk about it."

Two days earlier, Plater Robinson was covering a trial about one hundred miles farther south, in Jackson. A great clamor arose in the courtroom when the verdict was announced. "Thank God Almighty! We got justice at last." Thirty years afterward, a substantially more mixed jury than those in the 1960s, composed of both men and women, Blacks and whites, had just sent Byron De La Beckwith to prison for the rest of his days for the murder of Medgar Evers. The vote was unanimous. This white supremacist from Greenwood had been the primary suspect from the very beginning and had been judged twice in 1964 by juries composed entirely of white men, both trials ending in mistrial.

In theory, Roy Bryant wasn't in danger. Unlike the case of Byron De La Beckwith, a jury had pronounced on his case in 1955, and he could not be retried for the murder of Emmett Till. As for the abduction, he had never been tried, much less convicted, but the statute of limitations for that crime had expired; at the time, the authorities had only a two-year window to bring charges in Mississippi. Nevertheless, the message had been delivered. In Mississippi, impunity had ended.

So it was better not to talk about the case than to reopen Pandora's box.

Six months later, when yet another journalist showed up wanting to write a series of articles on the Till case, Roy Bryant refused to discuss it. However, for two hours, Bryant sat with a cup of coffee and vented to David Holmberg of the *Palm Beach Post*, interrupting himself from time to time to greet his customers, both white and Black. "I never had any problem with blacks. Hell, I got some right here, I guarantee you, would fight for me in a minute . . . I don't mistreat blacks, and I don't let them mistreat me."

The discussion revolved around racial relations in general, as well as the riots and ransacking that had shaken Los Angeles two years earlier after police officers accused of beating young African American Rodney King had been acquitted. The voice of Roy Bryant hardened and he grew defiant. "I'll tell you what I would have done. I would have shot every S.O.B. who walked out of a store with something in their arms. You wouldn't have been a man if you hadn't. Would you?"

When the article appeared in September 1994, Holmberg briefly summarized his impressions of the old man seen in a snapshot taken on the fly, from a distance, leaning on the back of his pickup truck with his elbows. He described Bryant as "angry, defiant, and now dying himself." The third adjective was already out-of-date. Three days earlier, Roy Bryant had died in a Jackson hospital. Carolyn was at his bedside despite having remarried twice since their divorce, but did not want to attend the burial.

13
A COFFIN STILL OPEN

Emmett Till was dead. His killers were dead. But the case was still alive. In the mid-1990s, it was Keith Beauchamp's turn to launch into a documentary on the murder. Beauchamp was a young film producer from Louisiana who managed to locate several of the protagonists who were still living, including Willie Reed, one of the prosecution's star witnesses back in 1955.

After living in Chicago under his father's name for years, he faced Beauchamp's camera and repeated the basic contours of his testimony at the trial. But this time, he identified two of the Black men who'd been on board J. W. Milam's pickup truck, keeping an eye on Emmett Till. They were Levi "Too Tight" Collins, one of the possible suspects that the prosecution had been unable to locate at the time of the 1955 trial, and Joe Willie Hubbard, a farm laborer whose name had filtered into the Black press at the time.

The filmmaker also collected the account of a woman who had been part of the group of young people who had gone to the Bryant grocery store with Emmett Till. A neighbor of the Wrights, she told the filmmaker about watching several cars go past the night J. W. Milam and Roy Bryant came for Emmett. "I looked at the window and it was just like daylight. And I said, 'My Lord, look the cars!' but I didn't know where they were going. So, after time, I see this Black man get out of the car, went to the back and the white went to the front."

Henry Lee Loggins also spoke. He'd been one of the Black suspects sought unsuccessfully by the prosecution before the murder trial. It was a couple of historians from Alabama, David Beito and Linda Royster Beito, who first succeeded in tracking him down and asking him questions by telephone. Linda asked the questions to put him more at ease—her husband was white and she was Black—but they just got denials, a denial that Loggins repeated for posterity in a raspy voice in front of Keith Beauchamp's camera. "My name is Henry Lee Loggins and I am supposed to been involved with, uh, Emmett Till, uh, but I wasn't. [. . .] I can't figure out why that they had me involved when I know nothin' about nothin', no more than was told."

Beauchamp's film, *The Untold Story of Emmett Louis Till*, was premiered to the public at a screening in Greenwich Village, in New York, in mid-November 2002. On that evening, Mamie Till stood at the director's side. She made a short statement. "We have to keep telling the story to raise people's consciousness and until justice prevails." In her concern for fighting for continued remembrance, Emmett's mother had also spoken to another film director, Stanley Nelson, who was finishing his own documentary on the case at the same time—*The Murder of Emmett Till*. He'd also managed to connect with people who claimed to have witnessed the procession of the murderers at the barn in Drew or the scrubbing of the bloody pickup truck afterwards. He also had postcards printed with an image of Emmett Till on them and suggested the film-screening audience members send them to the Mississippi State District Attorney, demanding that the investigation be reopened.

Outside these interviews, Mamie Till had also decided to tell her own story. During this time, she met twice a week at home with Christopher Benson, a former editor in chief and lawyer for *Ebony* magazine. Sitting at the kitchen table with Benson over banana pudding, she listened to him read aloud the chapters of an autobiography in progress. Mamie Till's eyesight was failing and her health had deteriorated. In the year 2000, she had to use a wheelchair to cross the Edmund Pettus Bridge in Selma, Alabama, one of the landmarks of the fight for civil rights, at the head of a delegation led by President Bill Clinton. But her appetite for living and for struggling remained strong.

In late November 2002, a *New York Times* reporter who visited her at home, where photos of her son were on display, found her in the middle of cooking an opulent dinner to celebrate her birthday: turkey, beef roast, oyster dressing, gravy, mixed greens, collards, cabbage, macaroni and cheese, string beans, rutabagas, and sweet potato pie.

A half century after her son's murder, Mamie Till realized that some people still believed in some kind of judicial outcome. "It looks like Emmett is surfacing again," she said. She'd noted a January 6, 2003, telephone conference call with the Mississippi authorities, but it would never take place. On that very day, on the way to her three-times-a-week dialysis appointment, Mamie Till died of a heart attack at the Jackson Park Hospital in Chicago. She was eighty-one years old.

❖

The funeral took place five days later, on January 11. Mamie Till lay in a white coffin, dressed in white. The casket was covered with white flowers and a photo of her son. Several African American elected officials from Chicago came to offer their final respects, like Carol Moseley-Braun, the first African American senator in the history of the United States. The pastor Jesse Jackson, who had twice run for the Democratic nomination during presidential elections, delivered a speech in which he inscribed Mamie Till's name in a long line of Black women who had changed their country. Alongside militant abolitionists Harriet Tubman and Sojourner Truth, Ida B. Wells, who had reported on and publicly denounced lynchings, and Rosa Parks, there would always be Mamie Till, who had refused to let the victim of a murder sink into oblivion. "In many ways, the killers saw Till's death as a hole, but Mamie saw an earthquake, and she used the aftershocks of the earthquake to wake up and shake up a nation."

Congressman Bobby Rush, who represented Mamie Till's district, also gave a eulogy. "Her courage moved a nation and moved a world. She single-handedly opened our eyes and created a will to fight injustice, wherever it may be." In January 2003, a child of the Great Migration who had set out from Georgia to Chicago at the age of seven, Rush had just finished his fifth consecutive term in the United States House of Representatives—and not because his seat was uncontested. In late 2000, he'd defeated an ambitious Harvard graduate in a bitter primary challenge, a man who'd been just a child when Bobby Rush was an activist at the height of the Black Panther movement. In that primary, he inflicted a significant defeat on his challenger, which was the first and only loss his opponent—whose name was Barack Obama—suffered throughout his successful career.

For Bobby Rush, those five terms in office before Mamie Till's death were followed by ten more. In July 2023, sitting in the office of a modest Chicago church where he officiated as pastor, he had only been retired from politics for seven months. He announced his retirement—which he preferred to call a "return"—in the Roberts Temple, the church where Emmett Till's funeral had taken place. He had spent a good part of his final year in Congress working for the adoption of two texts that were deeply meaningful to him. One was the first federal antilynching law, the Emmett Till Antilynching Act, and the other the nomination of Emmett Till and his mother for the Congressional Medal of Honor. Once again, he was working to extend the work of Mamie Till. "Once that casket was open, nobody could ever set it down again. The casket is still open," he said in his raspy, sometimes imperceptible voice, the effect of a vicious cancer of the salivary glands.

Shortly after Mamie Till died, Bobby Rush began working on a resolution requesting that the government reopen the investigation into Emmett Till's murder. He wasn't the only one who supported making this happen. Only a few minutes after Mamie Till's funeral was announced the formation of a new organization, the Emmett Till Justice Campaign. Its leader, Alvin Sykes, had long been engaged in the struggle against judicial error. In late 2002, while doing other research, he'd happened upon an article describing hopes for reopening the Emmett Till case, hopes nourished especially by the Keith Beauchamp and Stanley Nelson documentaries.

Sykes, born in 1956, realized that the family had been waiting for almost a half century. Immediately, he contacted Mamie Till and told her how, twenty years before, he had found a way to retry the murder of one of his friends, a Black musician beaten to death with a baseball bat in a Kansas City public park the night Ronald Reagan was elected. The killer was acquitted by a white-only jury in a Missouri state court but was later convicted in a federal court and sentenced to life imprisonment. Alvin Sykes's dream was to have the federal courts take up the Emmett Till case too.

Normally, Emmett Till's death fell under the jurisdiction of the state of Mississippi. According to laws in effect at the time of the crime, the murderers would have had to take Till across state lines or else torture him in a national park to justify FBI involvement. But Alvin Sykes had unearthed a tip for a strategy, a judicial memo a quarter-century old, conceived to require a new FBI investigation into the assassination of President John F. Kennedy, even though the crime fell only under Texas jurisdiction. Basically, the document argued that the federal government could investigate a past crime at any time to determine whether it fell under federal jurisdiction, even if, in the end, this does not turn out to be the case or if the statute of limitations seems to have expired.

In this way, on February 6, 2004, for three hours, Alvin Sykes and Keith Beauchamp rolled out their arguments around a conference table in the federal court in Oxford, Mississippi. Some of the suspects, they said, might still be alive. Moreover, new witnesses had materialized, and the FBI had the right to conduct a new investigation, then communicate its conclusions to the local courts.

Facing one another across the table, the federal judges and those from the state of Mississippi were both intrigued and skeptical. Alvin Sykes had a backup to convince them. A few days earlier, he had promised he would bring along Simeon Wright, one of the witnesses present during the grocery store incident and the kidnapping. "Simeon is now nearly seventy but smart as a whip and has a vivid memory of all that happened."

Arriving from Chicago by car, Emmett Till's cousin was a flesh-and-blood representative of a family's pain. He had never forgotten the night when, paralyzed with terror, he'd wondered if he was having a bad dream or living a very real nightmare. He didn't know if the intruders were coming to send his cousin back to Illinois or to kill them all right then and there.

The meeting ended on an optimistic note. The authorities seemed to be interested in the case, while members of Congress and local elected officials from Chicago to New York—by way of Washington—ramped up their appeals for a new investigation.

Finally, what had long seemed unthinkable really happened. On May 10, 2004, R. Alexander Acosta, a young lawyer born in Florida of Cuban immigrants, who had been named attorney general charged with civil rights by President George W. Bush just a year earlier, took the podium in the Department of Justice's press room in Washington. "Federal prosecutors and FBI agents today are being assigned to investigate the Emmett Till murder in partnership with the district attorney's office and local law enforcement. Their findings will serve as the basis for any possible prosecution."

The announcement was made with little notice and hadn't really been expected. Attendance was sparse, the speaker was calm, without visible emotion, his voice almost monotone. However, his words already rang with a first—strong—conclusion. Police and the judiciary had failed to act in 1955, opening the door to a "gross miscarriage of justice," which it would be appropriate to correct. Half a century after the murder of Emmett Till, the case was officially reopened.

A LIFE THAT MATTERS (2004–2023)

14
THE DEAD SPEAK

Like everyone, FBI Agent Dale Killinger sometimes saw his memory rewrite the past. For a long time, this former ranger, nicknamed "Killer" in jest by his fellow soldiers, was convinced he still had bullet fragments in his right leg—probably traces of enemy fire from the day he parachuted out of a helicopter on the island of Grenada in October 1983, when Washington deployed troops in response to a putsch. When he accessed his medical file years later, he learned that his left leg was actually the one that had taken shrapnel.

Stirring up old memories was exactly the challenge that this Oxford, Mississippi bureau agent had been bracing himself for in spring 2004. He had been charged with evaluating whether the passage in time had reinforced or distorted memories, those of the remaining witnesses in the Emmett Till case.

Killinger and his colleagues in the FBI had just finished up a collaborative operation with the Drug Enforcement Administration (DEA). Operation "Dirty Pool" had been a three-year undercover investigation of a money-laundering network connected to drug trafficking in the South. The case had required setting up and managing a bar, bribing civil servants, and wiretapping, and had resulted in dozens of convictions, including of several police officers.

Going from present-day trafficking to a cold case from decades before seemed like a complete change of universe, shifting from a tentacular network of corruption to one of the most savage murders of the segregation era. But for the agent, it was primarily a criminal investigation with its share of suspects, witnesses, and material evidence, even though he was aware of what a burning issue it had been and remained in people's memories.

And yet, when he got started, he didn't know any details about the case. Though he'd been posted in Mississippi after graduating from the FBI academy, Killinger had been born a thousand miles to the north in Pennsylvania. Discovering an America where the question of skin color was omnipresent astounded him. For example, just asking for the recommendation of a barber would bring an answer like, "Go see John, that Black guy."

His initial reflex was to borrow the few books that the public library had on the murder. He was starting almost from zero. The official archives were extremely thin, and the transcript of the 1955 trial could not be found. Hugh Stephen Whitaker, the young researcher who had his master's thesis on the subject, had located a copy but then lost it when his basement flooded. After four months of searching, the FBI finally managed to lay their hands on a third- or fourth-"generation" carbon copy, typed out on onionskin paper in a pale blue ink difficult to decipher. Two employees from the agency practically wore out their eyes trying to produce a legible version.

At that point, the FBI could finally know, without having to base their case on newspaper articles that were necessarily abridged and otherwise imprecise, what witnesses had stated in their sworn testimony at trial. Beyond that, he discovered that there were also dozens of other people who had never been heard from because they'd been too young at the time, had never been contacted, or especially, had been too frightened.

Contrary to usual practices, Dale Killinger had obtained authorization to conduct interrogations outside Mississippi, if accompanied by an agent from the local FBI office. The investigation took him to Chicago, of course, but also to Seattle, Detroit, and Dayton. Though a certain number of witnesses had moved over the decades, many had not budged. Fifty years later, Robert Hodges, the teenager who had found Emmett Till's body, was still living and fishing in the same place.

To explore the Delta more efficiently, Killinger enlisted Lent Rice, a local guide and retired bureau agent, who had grown up in Sumner. Because they didn't have the power of subpoena, no one was obligated to talk to them. They often arrived without notifying people ahead of time so they could gauge the witnesses by their reactions. Some were stunned by this unexpected visit. "Holy smokes, man, I ain't never talked to the FBI before. This like watchin' TV." The tone of their conversations was usually relaxed.

They were there to have people go back through their memories, not tear out the truth by force. To put their witnesses at ease, the agents asked them to describe the Mississippi of their youth, give them a picture of the topography, the roads, the railroad tracks, and the stores. By design, they often minimized the importance of the investigation. The most probable outcome, Dale Killinger assured them, was that this would just lead to a report and not indictments, to say nothing of a trial. "I think we're basically bein' historians for whoever wanted us to do this."

And actually, the history seemed to have been written already. William Bradford Huie's sensational 1956 article had convinced a good part of America that two men, J. W. Milam and Roy Bryant, had acted alone to kidnap and kill Emmett Till. Little by little, the FBI assembled a jigsaw puzzle of testimonies that filled out the portrait of a lynching that had been committed by many more than just those two men and belied the first version of facts. Anyway, there proved to be little that was credible, logistically. To perform the tortuous series of events before dawn as described in *Look* magazine, the two men would have had to chew through one hundred fifty to two hundred miles on the back roads of Mississippi while also taking time for long torture sessions with their victim in a barn and digging up the fan that would act as ballast for his body—all that in the space of three hours.

Officially, apart from the story entrusted to *Look*, the two murderers had never wanted to go into detail on what had happened. That was confirmed by their widows and their children. In late summer 2004, the FBI grilled Horace Milam, one of the kids who had played cowboys and Indians in the courtroom during the Sumner trial. J. W. Milam's older son now lived on the Mississippi coast, next door to his mother.

He described with amusement how his father used to shoot bees with his Colt .45 and bluntly summed up the little his father had told him about the Till case: "Well, I said, 'Well, what got the kid killed?' He said, 'You don't walk into a white man's store and tell a man's wife that you ain't been fucked till I fuck you.' I mean, my old man, I mean, I know this, my old man was cryin' when he said it. So that ended, that ended his world. 'Cause him and Uncle Roy were both doin' pretty good at the time. And that's all he ever said about it—didn't say I put a gun to his head and shot him. He didn't say nothin'."

What he and his people didn't know was that, in reality, his father and his uncle had talked before their death. In June 2005, at a public library in South Chicago, Dale Killinger collected the memories of Bonnie Blue, an African American documentary filmmaker from Chicago. She claimed that she had never sounded like a Black woman, something that had come in handy. In the late 1970s, she had tricked J. W. Milam into recording three telephone interviews, all of which she had unfortunately lost in a flood.

According to the story that Milam told her, a late-night poker game doused with bootleg whiskey had degenerated into an expedition involving five other men, three whites and two Blacks, in addition to his half brother Roy. Emmett Till had allegedly been tortured in two different places, including the Drew barn, where he was most likely finished off. Two of the Blacks recruited for the operation had spread cotton seeds over the ground to hide the blood stains.

Another testimony, consistent with this, and just as unusual in its form, brought the other murderer's words to life. Luster Bayless, a local native who hitchhiked to Hollywood in the 1960s to enjoy a nice career as a costume designer, contacted Dale Killinger. He had in his possession a recording of Roy Bryant. In the mid-1980s, he'd headed a project relating to the Till case. It was a challenge, but not the kind to frighten a man who had spent ten years designing costumes for John Wayne and survived the chaotic filming of *Apocalypse Now* in the Philippines.

Once back in the Delta region of his childhood, Luster Bayless persuaded Roy Bryant to take a funereal tour of the places relating to the case and had his researcher, a young woman, record their conversations. She'd even taken a Polaroid photo of Bryant, thirty years after, in front of the family grocery store in Money. Bryant had not implicated anyone else, but he denied the story in *Look* magazine and admitted that the Drew barn had been one of the stops on Emmett Till's final night. After considering depositing their victim in front of a hospital, given his state, he and his half brother had allegedly decided "to put his ass in the Tallahatchie River." With a laugh, Bryant concluded, "I'm the only one who's living that knows . . . that's all that will ever be known."

Perhaps that was true for the murder itself, but not for what preceded or followed it. Direct witnesses confirmed to the FBI the greater-or-lesser involvement of Black men who were in the service of J. W. Milam. On the morning after the murder, passersby had seen two Black men near his pickup truck parked in front of the gas station in Glendora. One of them was standing beside it, the other sitting on a brown tarp in the back of the truck. Blood thick as jam was dripping onto the ground from the truck bed and attracting flies. J. W.

Milam had explained that he'd killed a deer, and when one of the passersby replied that this wasn't the season, he lifted the tarp briefly, without showing what it was covering, before spitting, "This is what happens to smart niggers . . ." Another witness confirmed that he and a friend had been paid thirty-five cents each to clean up the blood stains on the truck.

Little by little, the composition of the small group of killers and potential accomplices took shape. Among the possible Black participants or spectators, Henry Lee Loggins and Levi "Too Tight" Collins were cited again. They were the two suspects who couldn't be found at the time of the trial. Joe Willie Hubbard, identified by Willie Reed, was also mentioned, as well as two new names: Otha Johnson Jr., alias "Oso," and Johnny B. Washington. They were two small hands of the Milam–Bryant clan, who'd been suspected of helping J. W. Milam and Roy Bryant during the kidnapping. The first allegedly even confessed to his son before dying.

Among those close to the two half brothers, witnesses especially suspected their (half) brother Leslie Milam; their brother-in-law Melvin Campbell, a hot-headed heavy drinker (during FBI questioning, Carolyn Bryant maintained that he was the one who'd shot Emmett Till in the head); and Hubert Clark and Elmer Kimbell, two friends.

Kimbell himself had been on the front page of the newspapers a few months after the trial. In December 1955, while drunk, he had killed Clinton Melton, a Black gas station employee in Glendora, with two bullets to the head. Kimbell had gotten angry at Melton for filling up his tank when he had only asked for two dollars' worth of gas. Slightly wounded, he then ran off to get his friend J. W. Milam to take care of him. Three weeks later, the widow of the gas station employee accidentally drowned in a bayou at the steering wheel of her car. Claiming self-defense, Elmer Kimbell had been acquitted of the murder of Clinton Melton at the same court and by the same judge who had ruled in the murder of Emmett Till, but in a trial with much less media coverage.

On August 29, 1974, Frances Milam, Leslie's wife, called Pastor Macklyn Hubbell of the town's Baptist church to come over to her house in Cleveland, in the heart of the Delta region. Her husband was stretched out on the sofa and had only a few days to live. He had things to disclose. Twenty years earlier, he had, in fact, been involved in the murder of Emmett Till. "He wanted to

A LIFE THAT MATTERS

tell me because he perceived me to be a man of God. He was releasing himself of guilt. He was belching out guilt," the pastor explained to the journalist Wright Thompson years later.

The episode is evidence that the FBI investigation was turning up leads as unexpected as they were frustrating. Tongues were loosening, but often, years—even decades—too late. J. W. Milam and Roy Bryant were dead; so were their brother Leslie Milam, their brother-in-law Melvin Campbell, their friends Hubert Clark and Elmer Kimbell and their employees Levi Collins, Otha Johnson and Johnny B. Washington, all possible accomplices.

Though documentary filmmaker Keith Beauchamp affirmed after releasing his filmed investigation that five people involved in the murder were still alive, the FBI investigation focused on two suspects. The first was Henry Lee Loggins. At over eighty years of age, he continued to insist stubbornly on his innocence. He had not been on the kidnappers' pickup truck, or anywhere near it. He hadn't even seen it. If someone said they'd seen him, they were lying. J. W. Milam sometimes let him buy gas or supplies on credit and he was a good boss, except the time he accused him—wrongly, according to Loggins—of stealing scrap metal, which got him six months in jail.

Agent Dale Killinger tried hard to get him to confess, telling him that he would probably not be charged. "You go down, ah, sort of in history as a man who knew a little bit more and didn't tell it, or the man who was forced to do what he was told that he had to back then, or get killed. And then when he was confronted with it, he told the truth, painful as it is." No luck.

The other suspect was Carolyn Bryant. Agent Killinger met with her several times. A half century after Mose Wright's story of the "lighter" voice he heard during the abduction, two Black witnesses, teenagers at the time, had hinted at her possible involvement in identifying Emmett Till. A few days after the incident of August 24, 1955, one of them was going back up to Money, his arms full of jars of molasses and tobacco, when Johnny B. Washington, the Bryants' Black employee, threw him in a pickup truck with the couple and J. W. Milam on board. According to the adolescent, Carolyn Bryant studied him before declaring, "That's not the nigger. That's not the nigger boy." Thrown off the moving truck, the young boy lost a tooth.

Only a few hours before the abduction, Roy Bryant had also verbally assaulted a Black teenager who had come to the grocery store with his mother and uncle after just coming home from a vacation in Chicago.

Suspecting him of being the kid who had insulted Carolyn, he asked him what he'd been doing the preceding evenings. When the boy refused to answer, Bryant laid into his mother verbally, telling her that she should teach him some manners. Carolyn Bryant begged her husband to leave the young man alone. He was not the one they were looking for.

At their first meeting, she looked to Dale Killinger like a pleasant person, but crippled with remorse. Now at the age of seventy, Carolyn Bryant did not question her husband's or brother-in-law's guilt, but she denied any personal involvement herself. She repeated her testimony from the trial on the alleged assault and claimed that on the evening of the kidnapping, Roy had left and she hadn't seen him again until the next day.

Shortly thereafter, Killinger took a flight to Quantico, headquarters of the FBI behavioral unit. The experts there warned that, fifty years later, it would probably be very difficult to get any new information out of her, as it would be profoundly suppressed, but maintaining a connection might help. So, in the months that followed, Dale Killinger talked with Carolyn Bryant regularly, until she called him in the summer of 2005. New memories of the kidnapping had come back to her. Sitting in her rocking chair, she confided that her husband, her brother-in-law, and Elmer Kimbell had in fact come to the grocery store with Emmett Till on the night of August 28, 1955. She didn't recognize Emmett, and Roy Bryant had promised to take him back to his great-uncle's house.

15
ANATOMY OF A MURDER

In cold cases, the death of witnesses and variations in stories over time is one aspect of the problem; the disappearance of material evidence is another. The FBI had few pieces of material evidence to sink their teeth into. The fan used to ballast Emmett Till's body had disappeared; a resident of the region had recovered it in the mid-1970s, then, uneasy having it around, had thrown it away. The ring on the victim's finger could not be found. As for the Colt .45 that J. W. Milam had brought back from the war and which he was suspected of using to pistol-whip, then shoot Emmett Till, the investigators located it at the home of a Mississippi family who had inherited it. It was taken apart and examined from end to end, but the weapon revealed no usable fingerprints.

Dale Killinger took Willie Reed inside the Drew barn, and his fear at approaching the building echoed like a piece of evidence. But the barn had undergone construction work since then. No trace of blood could be detected, and the only bone fragments recovered were from animals. Even the area where the body had been discovered had changed, right down to the bends in the streams, forcing the investigators to request from the Secretary of Agriculture old aerial photos to locate the possible places where the body could have been submerged and fished out of the water.

But there was at least one element of material evidence the FBI wanted—and could—obtain. Certain that the body buried on September 6, 1955, at the Burr Oak Cemetery really was Emmett Till, he saw in its exhumation a way to quiet the wild rumors. In the mid-1990s, some of the last jurors still living continued to insist that the body found in the river was too big for Till's supposed age or that a Black teenager of fourteen years of age could not have had hair growing on his chest.

Convincing the people close to Till to grant permission for exhumation was complicated. They were divided over this question. One part of the family, supported by the Reverend Jesse Jackson, thought the FBI was just performing a publicity stunt on the coffin of a teenager.

A LIFE THAT MATTERS

The agency responded dryly, through the press, that it was there to conduct a complete, meticulous criminal investigation, not a historical exercise.

On June 1, 2005, Wheeler Parker and Simeon Wright, two of the survivors of the kidnapping, attended the disinterment of their cousin's casket. The police were posted around the cemetery at dawn, entrance gates were closed, and a large white tent was erected on the lawn to prevent television helicopters from filming the process. A priest pronounced a brief prayer and referred to the story of Lazarus, who had emerged from the tomb after four days. A backhoe set to work, first attacking the coffin of a World War I veteran, who was buried just a few inches from the grave of Emmett Till, to avoid damaging it. After that, they dug down to Emmett Till's coffin. Thirty minutes later, steel cables lifted it, packed with dirt, out of the grave.

The authorities had been warned to expect nothing more than bones. The water table was high, and coffins were subject to water infiltration. The gravediggers tilted the coffin slightly and drilled a hole in it to drain any water out. Then the casket was loaded onto a truck and transported to the office of the coroner under police escort. When the coffin was unsealed, the room filled with the odor of the chemicals used to embalm the body in 1955. On the glass panel, they could still see fingerprints left by the hundreds of tearful mourners who had attended the burial. Thanks to being embalmed, the body had not changed in fifty years. It was tortured, yet paradoxically intact.

At the time of the murder, no one had done a serious examination of the body. This time, the authorities had an autopsy performed, a scan, a dental examination, and a DNA analysis. From the femur, they took a mitochondrial DNA sample, the DNA which is transmitted only by the mother. This revealed significant correspondence with the DNA of Simeon Wright, whose maternal grandmother was also Emmett Till's great-grandmother. Obtaining 100% certainty would require obtaining a nuclear DNA sample from the corpse and exhuming one of his two parents to obtain a sample from them. That was judged to be unnecessary, since the corpse's estimated age corresponded to that of Emmett Till at his death and its dentition reflected the photos taken of the young man during his life.

The autopsy also confirmed that Emmett had suffered multiple fractures to the skull, to the left femur, to the thyroid cartilage, and to both wrists. Some of them were perhaps due to the postmortem shock when his body was thrown into the river. The lead fragments found in

A LIFE THAT MATTERS

the skull coincided with bullets from a Colt .45 used by the US Army. Direct cause of death: a burst of gunshot shot to the head at point-blank range.

When the coffin was opened, Joyce Chiles, the district attorney of Mississippi's Fourth Judiciary District, immediately recognized in his face the *Jet* magazine photo that a classmate had shown her when they were teenagers. Born a little before the affair exploded, she had alternated between school and cotton picking on a Delta plantation, then spent time in the Army, worked in penitentiary administration and the Mississippi Bureau of Narcotics, where she made undercover purchases with dealers. In 2003, she became the first woman and the first Black person elected attorney of her district, which included, in particular, Leflore and Sunflower Counties.

This magistrate, reputedly "tough on crime," didn't hesitate to provoke the Black organizations, stressing that between gang wars and trafficking of all types, a significant portion of her work consisted of investigating murders committed by Black people against Black people. "Who would have thought, thirty-five years ago, that we, as Blacks, would allow the KKK to hang their robes up and do their job for them?"

As expected at the beginning of the FBI investigation, the Emmett Till case had landed on her desk; no federal crime had been committed, it was up to the Mississippi judicial system to settle it. In spring 2006, Joyce Chiles received twenty-eight volumes of text, eight thousand pages of interrogations and expert testimonies summarized in a one-hundred–page report soon to be made accessible to the public, with the names of living people whited out but often still guessable. She promised to go through it line by line.

In the world of the American judiciary, people sometimes say that a district prosecutor could indict a ham sandwich. Dating from the mid-1980s, when used by Sol Wachtler, an influential New York judge, the expression emphasized the enormous influence, sometimes considered excessive, of the district attorney on the members of the grand juries, who were ordinary citizens charged with pronouncing on probable cause.

Joyce Chiles didn't like this expression, which implied it was district attorneys who decided indictments and not the evidence. She was clear with her superiors—she was determined to examine the case in depth and required that it be solid. She was not interested in recommending an indictment just for show. There would be nothing worse than ripping open scars with a highly publicized trial, only to have it end in acquittal or even a conviction reversed on appeal.

On February 22, 2007, the DA assembled nineteen jurors, most of them women, with Blacks and whites represented in almost equal numbers, to examine a series of cases listed on the Leflore County judicial docket. Among the cases, they learned at the last minute, was one of the most inflammatory cases in the state's history. They had been charged with determining, by qualified majority, whether charges could possibly be brought for the abduction and murder of Emmett Till.

The case for Henry Lee Loggins, too weak, had not been submitted. They would only pronounce on the question of Carolyn Bryant. Her varying statements had raised doubts. Given the statements of several witnesses, her presence at Mose Wright's house to identify Emmett Till on the evening of his murder seemed conceivable. But even so, it wasn't sufficient. The two-year statute of limitations for kidnapping had expired in fall 1957. To get a conviction, it would have to be for homicide. And for that, it would have to be proved that Carolyn Bryant, even though she had allegedly not harmed Emmett Till physically, had demonstrated criminal negligence by identifying him when she knew the young man's life was in danger.

Dale Killinger, charged with presenting the results of his investigation, thought the case made enough elements available to pursue this direction. His presentation to the grand jury concluded with the names of the two Black men Carolyn Bryant had not identified as Emmett Till to her husband in the days and the hours preceding the abduction. He pointed out that they were both still alive, while Emmett was dead.

The testimonies were there, but material proof was lacking. Among the jurors, some felt they were being expected to make an unpopular decision by choosing not to indict. They were convinced that the seventy-year-old woman knew more than she was saying, but they also didn't have enough evidence to send her before a court. Others figured that even if Carolyn Bryant had been involved, it was out of terror, including physical, of her husband and brother-in-law. One of the jurors, George Smith III, grandson of the sheriff who had arrested Milam and Bryant in 1955, summarized the general feeling: "That's fifty to fifty-five years ago. It's hard to put something together when it was that long ago. You can sit and 'what-if' all day long, but when you stick to the facts, there was just nothing there."

After an hour of debate, the grand jury returned a unanimous vote of "no bill," and nobody was indicted in the case. Agent Killinger fumed, while the prosecutor Chiles congratulated the grand jury for not letting themselves be dominated by their emotions.

Notified on the way to his morning prayers, Simeon Wright was exasperated but not surprised. "You are looking at Mississippi. I guess it's about the same way it was fifty years ago. We had overwhelming evidence, and they came back with the same decision."

This time it was certain: Judicially, the Emmett Till murder case was closed.

16

THE CONFESSION THAT COULDN'T BE FOUND

"Dear Mom and Dad, I have arrived in Meridian, Mississippi. This is a wonderful town, and the weather is fine. I wish you were here. The people in this city are wonderful, and our reception was very good. All my love, Andy."

In his office adorned with a deer trophy, a rifle, and a gold judge's gavel, Jim Hood, Mississippi Attorney General from 2004 to 2020, kept the yellowed relic in a glass case: the last letter written by a man condemned to death without knowing it. It was signed Andrew Goodman, one of the three activists assassinated a few hours later on June 21, 1964, near Philadelphia, Mississippi. In that region, the case was sometimes referred

A LIFE THAT MATTERS

to as the *Mississippi Burning* case, from the title of the film starring Gene Hackman and Willem Dafoe as FBI agents who were pursuing the killers.

During his four terms of office, two cold cases linked to the civil rights movement had kept Jim Hood's days especially active. For sixteen years, the *Mississippi Burning* case and the Emmett Till case were like batons passing back and forth. Reopening the Till case in May 2004 had also amplified the hopes of those who were pushing for a new investigation into the case in Philadelphia, Mississippi. It was a hope fulfilled. In June 2005, the same month Emmett Till's body was disinterred, Jim Hood himself stood before a jury and successfully called for a sentence of sixty years in prison for Edgar Ray Killen, a Baptist pastor and recruiter for the KKK, who had been convicted of deciding and organizing the triple murder. It was one of the rare cases, he confessed today, where he could see something in a defendant that gave him goose bumps, some kind of evil aura.

At the time, the conviction of this octogenarian in a wheelchair, an oxygen tube up his nose and a nurse at his side, was seen by some as a promising omen for the Emmett Till case. The age of the accused didn't matter, the state of their health didn't matter—justice would triumph in the end. For others who were clear-eyed, this looked more like a possible last stand of Southern justice penalized by the disappearance of suspects, witnesses, and evidence.

Still today, Jim Hood conceded in his deep, rich voice, in the case of the Emmett Till murder, accomplices had probably avoided the worst. "I'm sure that there were other people involved in it that weren't prosecuted. But I guess the justice will be at the pearly gates when they have to justify themselves with the good Lord," concluded this practicing Baptist.

The remark was valid for the *Mississippi Burning* case as well. For ten long years after Killen was convicted, the justice system searched for possible accomplices who might still be living. The investigation was permitted by the Emmett Till Unsolved Civil Rights Crime Act, a 2008 law allocating permanent funds for this type of investigation.

In summer 2016, Jim Hood finally closed the case for lack of suspects to pursue. But it seemed like a major cold case would have to occupy the prosecutor's desk to the very end. Six months later, he said, "the media went nuts." In the last days of January 2017, reporters suddenly started harassing him with questions about the Emmett Till case. They wanted to know if the office was ready to reopen the investigation. It seemed that

A LIFE THAT MATTERS 163

ten years after he'd closed the case, Carolyn Bryant had revised her version of the facts.

This nth unexpected development had roots dating back almost a decade. In fall 2008, historian Timothy Tyson from Duke University rang the doorbell at a house in Raleigh, North Carolina. The owner had called to tell him that for Christmas, she'd given a copy of Tyson's most recent book, *Blood Done Sign My Name*, to her mother-in-law, who had very much appreciated this investigation into the murder of a young Black man in 1970, committed by a white merchant, his son, and his stepson, who'd accused the victim of insulting the son's wife.

The case had haunted Timothy Tyson, who, as a child, had lived on the same street as the men who'd been charged, and been friends with one of the sons. One day, while in college and writing a paper on the case, Tyson visited his childhood friend and heard his father let loose a remorseless confession: "That nigger committed suicide, wanting to come in my store and four-letter-word my daughter-in-law." Tyson decided to become a historian that very moment.

Tyson was thrilled by the praise from this unknown reader, but did not necessarily feel pressed to meet her. Until the voice on the other end gave her mother-in-law's name. "You probably know about her. Her name is Carolyn Bryant." He knew Bryant had spoken to no other journalist since her appearance at the Sumner trial. In terms of historical investigation in the South, it was the scoop of the decade, several decades, even.

The meeting took place over pound cake at the home of Carolyn's daughter-in-law Marsha. The son of a Methodist pastor, Timothy Tyson felt like he was meeting someone he could have run into at church. She could even have been an old aunt. In any case, she seemed to be approachable, but manifestly, she was struggling with the truth. As she sipped her coffee, Carolyn Bryant admitted to having gone over and over the events of late August 1955 in her mind, asking herself again and again who had done what.

"They're all dead now, anyway," she murmured, as if talking to herself before admitting that one part of her testimony at the trial, the part where Emmett Till had grabbed her by the waist and made obscene propositions, was not true.

Stupefied, Tyson struggled to form the following question: If that's not true, then what did happen?

A LIFE THAT MATTERS

"Honestly, I just don't remember. It was fifty years ago. You tell these stories for so long that they seem true, but that part is not true." Whatever happened, she concluded, "Nothing that boy did could justify what happened to him."

Timothy Tyson chose to make this the opening scene in his book, *The Blood of Emmett Till*, without, however, grasping the importance of this admission and without informing the authorities. For him, Carolyn Bryant had lied at the 1955 trial, that much was clear, but judicially, the case was closed. Anyway, he was a historian, not a journalist, and more interested in long-term work than by the noise of current events.

Almost ten years later, however, his revelations would make noise, to the point of briefly piercing the media frenzy during the hectic beginnings of the first Donald Trump presidency. Early reviews of the book, published in regional daily newspapers, did not capture the juiciest part of his work. The bomb didn't explode until *Vanity Fair* got hold of it in late January 2017. Carolyn Bryant had gone back on her version of the case. A few days later, the Till family called for a new investigation into her possible lies relating to the incident at the grocery store. And perhaps something even more serious.

More than ten years after the 2007 "no bill," an FBI agent went back to speak to Carolyn Bryant, as well as her daughter-in-law Marsha. Yes, they acknowledged, they had, in fact, met the historian. But Carolyn insisted that she had never gone back on her initial statements made at the 1955 trial and then to the FBI in 2004. The only reason she wasn't suing Timothy Tyson for defamation was to avoid having to make more statements in a courtroom. For his part, Tyson stood by his work.

The two women also stated that the interviews were supposed to feed plans for an exculpatory autobiography to be titled "I Am More Than a Wolf Whistle," which would be based on memories that Carolyn recounted to her stepdaughter, and that they didn't realize that Tyson had been planning to write his own book. Tyson said that he had never accepted such a project but had only given her a little general advice on the ruthless world of publishing.

Once again, investigators sifted through the labyrinth of contradictory declarations. Once again, material evidence was lacking. Timothy Tyson said he had committed to Carolyn Bryant that he would deposit the transcript of their conversations in the archives at the University of North Carolina, where they would remain inaccessible to the public until 2038. So, the FBI issued

A LIFE THAT MATTERS

a subpoena to obtain them and received the recording of an interview, two transcriptions of interviews, a page of handwritten notes, and a copy taken from a hard drive.

If Carolyn Bryant had uttered her retraction into a microphone, then the recording had been lost or erased, without having been transcribed. No audio or written trace of such remarks printed in the book existed on the tapes or in the transcriptions. Perhaps the elderly woman had made this admission before he'd started taping. But if that was the case, why wouldn't he have tried to get her to repeat it into a microphone? The only evidence preserved was a few notes that Timothy Tyson had scribbled on the fly on a yellow legal pad. "Bryant... That part wasn't true . . . Fifty years ago. I just don't remember . . . Nothing that boy did could ever justify what happened to him." The rest of the sheet was empty.

Therefore, on December 6, 2021, the Department of Justice and the FBI were forced to announce the closing of the investigation to the Till family. Nothing, in almost five years, had allowed them to establish the credibility of Timothy Tyson's information. What Carolyn Bryant stated to him in 2008, like what she had really experienced or done in 1955, would remain a mystery.

17
RASHOMON IN THE DELTA

When Roy left that evening, Carolyn Bryant put her sons in her bed before going to wait in the kitchen in her pajamas and bathrobe. At the back door, stamping feet announced her husband's return. He wasn't alone. Behind him were J. W. Milam and another man, both of them holding a young Black man by the arms.

"We got him, but we want to be sure it's him. Is it him?"

"No, it's not him."

The young woman answered in a small voice without even glancing at the teenager's face. She tried to say it again with more conviction. "It's not him, you have the wrong person."

"Damn it, look at him, you haven't even looked at him!"

A LIFE THAT MATTERS

"No, it's not him. You have the wrong person, it's *not* him."

A strange smile suddenly flashed on the young man's lips, as if all this story had nothing to do with him. As if he was in no danger.

"Yeah, it was me."

In tears, Carolyn Bryant begged her husband to take him back home. The teenager had scared her, that's all; she had not been in danger. At first, Roy refused. "He could come back in the store and hurt you and I won't stand for that." She wore him down and finally he gave in. A few hours later, when he came home again, his clothes smelled of sweat and cigar. No trace of blood.

That was the story of the night of August 28, 1955, as Carolyn Bryant set it down in her planned autobiography. To the FBI, however, she'd delivered very different versions over the years. At first, she'd confirmed that her husband had gone off and she hadn't seen him again until the next morning. Later, she had acknowledged that he had come back with Emmett Till, but without ever mentioning the young man's confession.

This memory with gaps was also apparent in her memories of the August 24 incident at the grocery store. Those who have dissected it often evoke a *Rashomon* in the Delta, the title of the film by Akira Kurosawa in which a crime is recounted differently by four characters. Everyone agrees that Emmett Till whistled. According to his mother, it was probably to avoid stuttering. According to some witnesses, he was mocking a gross error by one of the checkers players on the front porch. For most of them, including Emmett's cousins, the young man, who was sure of himself and impulsive, really had whistled to greet Carolyn Bryant as she came out of the store. On the other hand, those present—to be sure, some of them close to Emmett Till, and not all of them attentive—had not remarked on any aggression through the window or felt any indication of one.

As for Carolyn Bryant, she varied her story of the minute, or handful of minutes, during which she was alone in the store with Emmett Till from the moment Wheeler Parker walked out onto the porch to the moment Simeon Wright walked in. At the 1955 trial, as in her autobiography, she declared that Emmett had grabbed her by the waist and had made emphatic and vulgar advances. There, too, a written trace cast doubt

A LIFE THAT MATTERS

on the dependability of her testimony on the stand, a three-page handwritten note, written by one of Roy Bryant and J. W. Milam's lawyers after an interview with "Mrs. Roy Bryant," two days after the discovery of the corpse, on September 2, 1955. The story it told was different. Mrs. Bryant said that Emmett Till really had taken her hand and suggested they go out, but that nothing else had happened before he walked out with a simple "Goodbye."

It was as if reality had slowly faded into a more or less fictional reconstruction as versions of the story were layered one on top of the other. When Carolyn Bryant described in her autobiography the moment when her husband's and brother-in-law's acquittal was announced, she recalled turning her head and briefly catching the eye of Mamie Till. Yet, the actual facts concerning that moment had been published in all the newspapers the very next day. Emmett's mother had already left. She'd seen the Black people in the audience leaving the courtroom with trepidation, early in the deliberations, having a feeling about the coming verdict. So Mamie didn't see the defendants hug their spouses and parade around with cigars in their mouths. She only heard on the radio of the jubilation in Sumner, like the local baseball team had just won the championship.

Through their successive versions of a story, actors in a court case can become deliberate or involuntary stage directors of themselves and others, sometimes to the point of incoherence. They can convince themselves of the veracity of a story that was sometimes constructed on shifting sands from the start. Juanita, who was J. W. Milam's widow, and close to Carolyn Bryant at the time of the murder, expressed this theory to the FBI in 2004. After showing little desire to talk about the case by limiting herself to answers like "I don't know" and "I don't think so," she had ended up wondering, in the presence of the investigators, if her sister-in-law might have exaggerated the story of the grocery store incident from the beginning.

"The only way I can figure it is that she did not want to have to take care of the store. She thought this wild story would make Roy take care of the store, instead of leavin' her with the kids and the store. That is a female point of view."

"You don't think it happened at all? She made it up? With Emmett Till?"

"Uhhh . . ."

"Just to get out of workin'?"

"He could have winked at her or whistled at her."

When this second investigation concluded, the FBI had not found probable cause to send Carolyn Bryant to federal court for perjury or false statements, but they maintained doubts on the reliability of her story of the case. Yet fifteen years after the 2007 dismissal, voices still continued to call on the Mississippi courts to bring charges against her and for a grand jury to determine whether she had knowledge of her husband's and brother-in-law's criminal plans or had indeed participated.

In midsummer 2022, when the contents of Carolyn Bryant's autobiographical manuscript leaked to the press, the *Chicago Tribune*, Illinois's largest daily paper, saw red. Once again, Carolyn Bryant was saying that she had done everything possible to save Emmett Till. Let her come tell that to a jury in a proper trial, "a fair one. Utterly unlike what was afforded to Emmett." At the beginning of August 2022, Leflore County again called a grand jury of citizens to debate the grounds for a possible trial in light of these most recent developments in the case. Seven hours of hearings to reach a decision that remained unchanged: Carolyn Bryant would not be indicted.

18
"SAY HIS NAME!"

At eighty years of age, Georgia Representative John Lewis had felt the end of his life drawing near. Before dying of pancreatic cancer on July 17, 2020, this veteran of the great battles of the civil rights movement had left a farewell letter to be published in the press on the day of his funeral. The final months of his life had taken him back to his youth. In the protests that had broken out in the spring, after the death of forty-six-year-old African American George Floyd at the hands of police during an arrest in Minneapolis, he heard echoes of the case that had rattled and enraged him at the age of fifteen. "Emmett Till was my George Floyd."

Fifteen years later, the second investigation of the Emmett Till murder had not ended with a guilty verdict any more than the first one. But the America of 2017–2022 was no longer that of 2004–2007. In 2008, the destruction of a historical marker on the case in Mississippi attracted little notice and inspired only modest donations. A decade later, the same kind of incident brought a deluge of articles and dollars.

The first FBI investigation took place in a nation that some imagined to be "post-racial," where the still little-known Barack Obama had established himself as the star orator at the 2004 Democratic convention proclaiming that there didn't exist a Black America and a white America and a Latino America and an Asian America, but only the United States of America.

The second FBI investigation began during the first days of the first Donald Trump presidency, which was marked by a steep increase in pessimism around racial questions. It ended with the return in force of protests against police brutality committed against Black people. Suddenly, the name of the teenager from Chicago was again heard at demonstrations, appended to one of the emblematic slogans of the Black Lives Matter movement: "SAY HIS NAME! EMMETT TILL!" The young man martyred in 1955 had become a figure of America in the present, and the criminal investigation into his death, a reflection of current interrogations. How do we get justice? What is justice?

Wheeler Parker is not directly related to Emmett Till by blood, yet he is. His maternal grandmother was the first wife of Mose Wright; Mose's second wife, Elizabeth Smith, was Emmett Till's great-aunt. Their blood ties date to the night of the kidnapping on August 28, 1955, the night of terror that sent the younger of the two cousins to his death and that rocked the fate of the cousin who was two years older.

In 1993, Wheeler Parker had become the reverend of the Argo Temple Church of God in Christ, a Pentecostal church in Summit, a small town on the edge of Chicago. This parish occupied a central place in the family's history, having been cofounded in the mid-1920s by Alma, Emmett's maternal grandmother. Emmett had lived his first ten years in Summit before he and his mother moved to Chicago. In 1947, the Parkers had arrived from Mississippi and moved in next door. Wheeler and his cousin and best friend often played together, messing around, including jumping onto slow-moving freight trains, then jumping off again several hundred yards farther down the track.

On this day in summer 2023, the church was busy and a choral group was rehearsing a gospel song with spirit. The reverend and I drove to the Emmett Till Memorial Center, a community center nearby. On his black robe, he had pinned a Juneteenth badge to mark the June 19 anniversary of the federal government intervention of 1865, which forced Texas to respect the Emancipation Proclamation that had freed the enslaved. A number of states later made it a holiday while the country was torn apart over its history.

Certain politicians, in a desire for supposed national glory, wanted to tear out or conceal the less glorious pages of United States history. These included the Emmett Till murder case. Wheeler Parker had already heard high school students tell him that if something had happened to his cousin, he must not have been completely blameless. In a different iteration, some parents didn't want their children to learn about this episode because they thought America could now leave it behind. "It's a hard story to tell, to sell, the story's not pleasant. It doesn't fit white Americans' vision and idea about black people."

Wheeler Parker felt the complex emotions of a country that had progressed but could sometimes be galling. A nation where the Black condition had improved but where racism remained significant. He grasped the anger of the younger generations, but had trouble making them see the America of his youth, the nation of all-powerful segregation. The universe where, for example, one of his uncles had been threatened with having the tongue cut out of his mouth for contesting the accounts of the white planter, who, knowing he enjoyed complete immunity, had calculated his own share of the cotton harvest to the uncle's disadvantage. "They don't know nothin' about what I'm talking about. All they see is this is a racist country and you're an Uncle Tom."

Wheeler Parker recognized the police brutality and injustice in the courts, but ultimately, he had never given up faith in the system. When a grand jury again refused to indict Carolyn Bryant in the summer of 2022, he didn't condemn the authorities. Unlike other members of the Till family, he thought Dewayne Richardson, the prosecutor charged with the case and an African American, had done his best. Sitting next to him, journalist and lawyer Christopher Benson, one of the official spokespersons for the family, summarized Parker's behavior with a catchphrase. "Wheeler was after the truth, but he certainly would have wanted Carolyn Bryant to be arrested. The younger people wanted her arrested, and then they wanted the truth."

❖

Priscilla Sterling belonged to that younger generation. This fifty-something distant cousin of Emmett Till lived in Mississippi. In the trunk of her car parked near the Civil Rights Museum in Jackson, a brown building with angular facade joined to a more traditional museum housing the history of Mississippi, she kept protest signs. They included an image that mobilized the civil rights activists across the state at that time: the face of Michael Corey Jenkins, a young Black man shot in the mouth in March 2023 during a police search conducted by ten police officers without a warrant.

Priscilla Sterling had always known she was part of the Emmett Till family, but the subject had never been mentioned at home. She had attended an integrated school where the white children were a large majority. "I was just thinking, that stuff happened way back then and that doesn't happen now." It took experiencing racism for herself, as an adult, and her discussions with Mamie Till to motivate her to dive into the old family papers and then go explore the Delta. She started following the case with a watchful eye in the early 2000s, and she refused to consider the case closed after the two grand juries declined to bring charges against Carolyn Bryant.

"Wheeler doesn't feel like I do. Wheeler kind of didn't want her to go to jail. And let me tell you now, and I'm going to be honest, it killed me to literally say that I wanted her to be prosecuted and go to jail. Because I looked at my mama and I'm like, I don't want my mama in jail. And then all of a sudden, I thought about justice. Well, she can be in the bed and they can accommodate her room, but just to show the world that you can't get away with being a part of a kidnapping and murder."

For her, whether or not those responsible for those new official investigations had been eager to find the truth, the process had been tainted from the start. The way Mississippi was still governed today, it was impossible to obtain justice.

19
THE END OF THE TRAIL

When a subject captivates America, Hollywood likes to produce related fictional accounts in duplicate. What is true for volcanic eruptions or asteroids falling from the sky has also held true for the Emmett Till case. In January 2022, ABC broadcast *Women of the Movement*, a series filmed in the Delta that focused on the struggle of Mamie Till. Nine months later, a full-length film was released to movie theaters. Titled *Till*, it had been filmed in Georgia and coproduced by Keith Beauchamp, the author of the documentary *The Untold Story of Emmett Louis Till*.

In February 2023, the White House organized an official projection of the film in the East Room, where they handed out popcorn and packets of tissues under the chandeliers and amidst the gold trim. At the podium, before the lights were turned out, President Joe Biden recalled the atrocities of segregation. "Innocent men, women, and children, hung by nooses from trees. Bodies burned and drowned and castrated. Their crimes? Trying to vote. Trying to go to school. Trying to own a business or preach the Gospel. False accusations of murder, arson, and robbery. Simply being Black."

This event shows that the Till case has penetrated the national conscience. Seventy years after the Eisenhower administration's inaction, it is recognized here at the highest level. It was chosen as an example of the dark moments of American history by an aging president who'd received strong support from Black elected officials during his victorious campaign of 2020, but who, fifty years earlier, had also been a young senator from Delaware being mentored by his old segregationist colleague Jim Eastland from Mississippi, the man who had leaked Louis Till's military file to discredit the Till family. "What can good ol' Jim Eastland do for you in Del'uh'weah?" he asked Biden with solicitude over a whiskey on the threshold of a difficult campaign.

The importance of the Till case was acknowledged, but there was no consensus on the course of events. The

Till project had been supported by several members of the family, including Priscilla Sterling. *Women of the Movement* had been approved by others, including Wheeler Parker.

The series highlighted the work of the jurists who had tried unsuccessfully to have Roy Bryant and J. W. Milam convicted in 1955, especially prosecutor Gerald Chatham.

The film, on the other hand, more concise by nature, focused on the mother, the heroine who was up against a monolithic and crushing system of white supremacy. *Till* affirmed without ambiguity Carolyn Bryant's responsibility in the abduction. We see her identify the young man from inside the abductors' car. *Women of the Movement* is a little more allusive. The series reduces this key character to a voice in the dark, a voice "lighter" than a man's, as Mose Wright had testified.

Storms had always broken out among the defenders of the memory of Emmett Till. Already in autumn 1955, Mamie Till, who was touring the United States to recount her son's ordeal, and the NAACP, which was using her testimony to keep the activist flame alive, abruptly halted their collaboration over financial disagreements. Thus, there was nothing new in the proliferation of slightly dissonant stories regarding the case in the mid-2020s or the acid judgments expressed by some of the actors concerning others, whether members of the family, investigators, or experts.

Questions are still being asked, not only about the story but also about who is telling the story, who has a right to tell it, how, and to what end. People wonder who can claim the progress that it has engendered and who must shoulder the disappointed hopes, perhaps excessive, of the twenty-first-century investigations. To what extent did the judicial system play all its cards in 1955, in 2007, and in 2022, and to what extent did it fold too quickly? In the end, to what extent does the long life of this case symbolize progress in America—or what has *not* changed?

In addition to the two works of fiction, these differences of opinion are embodied in an old sheet of paper. On June 21, 2022, a team of budding detectives, including Deborah and Teri Watts, two distant cousins of Emmett Till, along with director Keith Beauchamp, showed up at the Leflore County Courthouse in Greenwood. In the past, the sheriff's office and the jail had been housed in the basement. Today, those spaces are filled with dozens of archive boxes, which are covered with cobwebs and dust, and organized chronologically.

The decade is written on each box with faded green or black magic marker. Donning gloves and masks, clambering up on chairs to reach the highest shelves, the little band of judicial archaeologists unearthed what they had come in search of: a warrant for the arrest of Roy Bryant and J. W. Milam, yes, but also Carolyn Bryant—for kidnapping. And it had been signed by a judge. It was dated Monday, August 29, 1955, the day after the abduction and two days before Emmett Till's body was found in the river. When Keith Beauchamp read it, he felt the presence of Mose Wright, who had come to the courthouse to denounce them that day and was accusing them, still, from beyond the grave.

The existence of this warrant had been no secret at the time. It was just that County Sheriff George Smith, out of a case of paternalism, had decided to leave Carolyn Bryant out of the case. "We aren't going to bother the woman. She's got two small boys to take care of," he said to reporters. Accordingly, one page of the document bears his signature and mentions the arrest of the two suspects with this laconic note: "Mrs. Roy Bryant not found in my county." Present at the grocery store when her husband was questioned on Sunday afternoon,

August 28, Carolyn had been spirited away by the Milam–Bryant clan that very day to avoid scrutiny.

For some members of the Till family, this was an archive of historic importance, but it had no judicial utility. Carolyn Bryant had already been heard from several times since 1955, and the statute of limitations had expired on the crime of abduction long before. However, those who discovered the warrant claimed that it provided an opening in the case. Maybe a new chance to question the old woman and to see her crack finally.

For several months, activists dreamed of using the warrant themselves against the person they'd been considering a suspect at large. The hunt for her first went through Raleigh, North Carolina, in July 2022. A few dozen activists assembled with signs showing a recent photo of Carolyn Bryant, topped with the word WANTED in large capitals on a red background. They targeted an apartment, then a retirement home. "Time to face your demons. Come on out!" In the end, the police had to intervene.

In early December 2022, they tried again, this time in Bowling Green, Kentucky, in front of the county courthouse, then in front of what was said to be Carolyn Bryant's last-known residence. In midsummer, the *Daily Mail,* a British tabloid specializing in eye-catching headlines and paparazzi photos, published pictures of an old woman with gray hair, an oxygen tube in her nose, and her shih tzu dog on a leash. She was receiving care for an advanced-stage cancer and living in a small apartment in the "Bluegrass State."

Several African American activist organizations, some controversial, like the New Black Panther Party or the Lion of Judah Armed Forces, made the trip there. The demonstrators received anonymous threats, forcing the city to postpone its Christmas parade. Some of the demonstrators arrived with assault rifles over their shoulders. Their tract emphasized that the First Amendment to the Constitution, guaranteeing the freedom of speech, went nicely with the Second Amendment, which guaranteed the right to have well-organized militias.

Priscilla Sterling, who was there, thanked those attending. "I just want you all to know that it was white supremacy that freed Carolyn Bryant, that freed J. W. Milam, that freed Roy Bryant." Eventually, in February 2023, Emmett Till's cousin filed a complaint against the sheriff of Leflore County for failing to execute a warrant for arrest.

The search came to an end in Louisiana on April 25, 2023. That day, Carolyn Bryant died in Westlake at the age of eighty-eight, a few dozen miles from where she had buried her oldest son in 1995. Amid the expressions of outrage or duly recording the information with administrative neutrality, the Reverend Wheeler Parker, while deploring that the death of his cousin had gone unpunished, expressed his unexpected reaction: pity. "Our hearts go out to the family of Carolyn Bryant Donham. As a person of faith for more than sixty years, I recognize that any loss of life is tragic and don't have any ill will or animosity toward her."

Priscilla Sterling remarked that, at first, she hadn't believed Carolyn Bryant had died and briefly wondered if it wasn't one last ruse before acknowledging the reality. "I hope her soul rests in peace because I'm not God," she says today. "She's gone now. That's between her and God."

Of all the participants in the 1955 trial—defendants, judge, prosecutors, lawyers, jurors, and witnesses—Carolyn Bryant was the last to die.

EPILOGUE

THE STATUES' GAZE

Route 49 crosses all of Mississippi, from the Gulf of Mexico to the Arkansas border, splitting into two branches as it crosses the Delta. The eastern section, Route 49E, renamed Emmett Till Memorial Highway, leads to most of the landmarks related to the case. In an ironic geographical twist, 49E intersects with a section of State Highway 32, named in honor of Sheriff H. C. Strider, in the village of Webb, where Mamie Till was born. The western section, Route 49W, crosses Sunflower County, and here, there is no visible marker dedicated to the memory of the lynched teenager. Route 49W does, however, give access to one of the essential locations in the case.

Drive for a few miles west from Drew, over a pocked road through the countryside, then turn onto a small, unpaved road that opens onto a bucolic landscape. Behind a bayou, slightly elevated and overlooking vast lawns, is a house with a swimming pool flanked by two barns. The larger barn serves as a garden shed for the family that has lived there for several decades without knowing anything about the place at first. They welcome people who want to spend a little time there to reflect or transmit the memory. It is there that, according to the FBI investigation, Emmett Till was tortured for a long period of time on the night of August 28, 1955.

On one side of the bronze podium, the sculptress has reproduced in bas-relief the bloodied barn in Drew, which sits behind a foreground of cotton blossoms. On the other side, a crowd of mourners surround the coffin of Emmett Till on the day of his burial. The podium is adorned with a photo of the young boy from Chicago at the age of ten. Behind the podium stands Mamie Till, her left hand stretched out, palm up, as she addresses the crowd.

EPILOGUE: THE STATUES' GAZE

Ollie Gordon arranged to meet me in front of this monument in Summit, Illinois, dedicated to Emmett Till's mother and erected a few hundred yards from the Argo Temple. The statue's eyes are fixed on the Argo Community High School, the city's public high school, a red, brown, and yellow brick building. Mamie was one of its first Black graduates. The students call themselves the Argonauts and the street leading up to it is bordered with signs reading "I am Argo." That is the name of the neighborhood, but especially what allowed people to earn a living for a long time. The Corn Products Refining Company's largest corn-processing factory in the world was there in Summit, extracting Karo Syrup, Mazola Oil, and Argo Corn Starch. Emmett Till's maternal grandfather and father were employed there as factory workers.

Ollie Gordon's family also came north from Mississippi toward Chicago in the early 1950s to improve their daily life. For a time, she lived on the first floor of the Till house on the South Side. Her cousin Emmett, who was seven years her senior, and his mother occupied the second floor. "Emmett was more a sibling than a cousin. He was like an older brother, very protective. He was a prankster, he liked to make people laugh, but he was very responsible, very helpful at home. His mom let him take the bus to go downtown paying groceries, paying bills. He said to her, 'Mama, if you can go out making money, then I can be responsible for the house.'" The death of her cousin marked the first time she'd experienced grief. A house that had always been joyful was suddenly darkened with adults' tears and children's nightmares.

Ollie Gordon's daughter, Airickca Gordon-Taylor, who died in March 2020 at the age of fifty, was buried in the same cemetery as her cousin under the epitaph WARRIOR FOR CIVIL RIGHTS, SEEKER OF JUSTICE FOR EMMETT LOUIS TILL. In the summer of 2013, the words "Black Lives Matter" began to circulate on social media after George Zimmerman, a neighborhood watch volunteer in Florida who was accused of shooting seventeen-year-old Trayvon Martin, was tried and acquitted. Overcome with anger, Airickca Gordon-Taylor demonstrated in Chicago. "When I heard the verdict, I said, Wow! This is what this must have felt like fifty-eight years ago. [. . .] The wound is still there, unhealed."

In the years that followed, Airickca Gordon-Taylor spoke publicly alongside families in their struggle against police brutality and formed "a support system, a club you don't want to belong to," as her mother phrased it.

EPILOGUE: THE STATUES' GAZE

"These families needed some way to understand: Where do I go from here? How do we deal with this?" These families were in a quest for meaning in the death of their child, meaning that Emmett Till's mother had found. "His mother always said that was his life journey, that he had to die in order to open up the doors to the world so they can see all the injustice and the lynchings that have been going on for generations."

In the beginning, this statue of Mamie Till was supposed to be a bust, but in the end, the decision was made to represent her standing before the court, telling her story, as she'd done in 1955 and until the end of her life. The monument was inaugurated on April 29, 2023, four days after the death of Carolyn Bryant. No one mentioned her passing.

In the corners of the small plaza where the statue was erected, there are four concrete cylinders topped by plaques. Each one mentions a location that is significant to the case: the Till's house, just three hundred yards away; the Roberts Temple in Chicago, ten miles away; the Tallahatchie County Courthouse in Sumner, nearly five hundred sixty miles from there; and Washington, DC, six hundred miles away. These are the places where Emmett Till had grown up, where his funeral was held, where two of his murderers were wrongfully acquitted, and where the US congressmen had voted for laws that bear his name. Four places whose status is clear, whose relation to this complex case is well established historically. That is far from being the case for all of them.

In late July 2023, President Joe Biden proclaimed the establishment of a national monument to honor Emmett Till and his mother. The decision placed three symbolic locations relating to the case under the protection of the federal government, like so many other historical or touristic sites, from the Mariana Trench to Mount Saint Helens, to the Statue of Liberty, to the battlefield of Little Bighorn.

The first of the three places, the Roberts Temple in Chicago, has been awaiting restoration for years. The second, the Sumner courthouse, was renovated in 1973, as if in an effort to erase the shame of the 1955 trial. In 2015, a reverse operation took place. The courtroom was

EPILOGUE: THE STATUES' GAZE

restored to its state sixty years before: same chairs, same tables, same windows, even the same tobacco spittoons installed at the entrance. But there was one major change made. Behind the judge's podium, the Mississippi flag had previously been adorned with a Confederate flag motif. That had been changed by referendum. The flag behind the podium now displayed the state flower, the magnolia.

When it was time to choose a third location, there were not that many options. In Drew, the barn, the site of torture, stood on private property. Mose Wright's house in Money had long disappeared, demolished by a tornado. All that remained were the white ruins of the little church nearby where Emmett's great-uncle had done his preaching and the cemetery where Emmett had almost been buried, which was a tangle of weeds.

Of course, the activists of Emmett's memory would have liked to recover the Bryant grocery and preserve the ruins like a symbol of the efforts to erase the case, or build a place of teaching and dialogue there. But the little that remained of the commerce was held by descendants of Ray Tribble, the youngest member of the jury that had acquitted Roy Bryant and J. W. Milam. They demanded an exorbitant price.

With a mastery approaching cynicism, these inheritors had, on the other hand, managed to land a government grant to restore the neighboring service station, justifying it by its supposed historic value. Anyone who pauses to contemplate the ruins of the Bryant grocery store now is confronted with an ersatz "new" structure, just a few feet away, one right out of an Edward Hopper painting, with old-fashioned gas pumps and vintage advertisements for orange soda and cigarettes.

Since the location of the incident between Emmett Till and Carolyn Bryant was a private property, the location of the kidnapping destroyed, the location of the murder imprecise, another site, the third one, was finally dedicated. Its status is also unclear, its history tormented. It is a riverbank nicknamed Graball Landing, near the village of Glendora. According to local folklore, long ago, the children of families who came to a cotton plantation to buy food were invited to dig into a big burlap sack and *grab all*—as many pieces of candy as they could. The place was bequeathed to the federal government by the Sturdivants, an important family in the region, the family who had rented Leslie Milam the property where Emmett Till was tortured in 1955.

EPILOGUE: THE STATUES' GAZE

Since 2008, two mauve signs have been guiding the visitor to the riverbank where, apparently, Emmett Till's body was pulled from the river, or more or less—within a few miles. The exact location is still murky. But since then, Graball Landing has also become a symbolic place in the Till case as a duty to memory, always contested. Several times, the markers have been vandalized, like others commemorating the case in other locations. They have been spray-painted in red with the letters KKK, squirted with acid, shot up with bullets, uprooted, or thrown in the river.

One winter night, in 2019, three members of the Kappa Alpha fraternity, an organization founded under the sponsorship of Confederate General Robert E. Lee, had their pictures taken in front of the signs, all smiles, and brandishing semiautomatic rifles. The signs had been damaged by a dozen bullets. Without convincing anyone, their lawyer explained that they were only carrying these weapons to trample the grass and drive out the snakes. The students were not sanctioned either by their university or by the law. The following fall, militants from the League of the South, a nationalist organization, arrived dressed in black turtlenecks and military trousers, waving Confederate flags in front of the signs. This was captured by surveillance cameras.

Long deserted by its last white residents, Glendora, though one of the poorest villages of one of the poorest regions in one of the poorest states in the United States, houses a small museum dedicated to the Emmett Till case in the warehouse where the murderers had procured the cotton gin fan. Today, it is the Emmett Till Historic Intrepid Center.

Johnny B. Thomas, the mayor since 1982, is a local character, often at war with the power structures he considers his persecutors, especially since he spent several months in prison for illegal deployment of slot machines in his café. "I look at the President now that's going through what poor people like myself has always been. I'd like to say to him "I understand how you feel". Now, anytime that he sees a police car coming by, he think whether they're coming after him," he says, flashing a smile, a few days after Donald Trump's nth indictment. He intends to use the Emmett Till case to help his community climb out of poverty, even if it means leaning on history that is still unverified.

Glendora claims that Till's body was thrown into the river from the Black Bayou Bridge, a rust-colored trestle

EPILOGUE: THE STATUES' GAZE

bridge, now decommissioned, and that the murderers had stolen the cotton gin fan that acted as ballast from his warehouse. "We are a food desert here. Our effort here was to grow sweet potatoes and we could not make a success of it, and we decided to grow our history," the mayor remarked.

Johnny B. Thomas maintains a personal relationship to the case. His father—or stepfather—was Henry Lee Loggins, a suspected accomplice of Roy Bryant and J. W. Milam until his death in 2009. His mother, Adeline Hill, worked at King's Place, the juke joint in Glendora, "the Las Vegas of the plantation," and was one of journalist James Hicks's favored sources during his hunt for witnesses before the trial.

At the time of the FBI investigation, Johnny B. Thomas was convinced that Loggins had indeed aided the murders and hoped he would confess in exchange for immunity. But that didn't happen. For him, Glendora embodies the opposite of Sumner in the Till case. In Sumner, the whites acquitted one another, then much later expressed regrets when Tallahatchie County apologized to the Till family in late 2007. In Glendora, Blacks who were no longer enslaved but were still subjugated had been coerced, at the risk of reprisals, into collaborating in a murder. Hence, the qualifier "intrepid," in homage to the audacity of Mose Wright during the trial and the bravery of Mamie Till throughout her life.

The memory of Emmett Till, in Glendora as in the Delta region generally, is still being constructed, still in flux, raw. It is present everywhere, yet fragmented, like Route 49, agitated by ebbs and flows, just like the rivers. It's both public and private, made of places that have been degraded or erased by the time, while others are renovated or new.

It took many years to see a statue of Emmett Till erected there. The first idea was to erect it in front of the Leflore County Courthouse in Greenwood, the place where, in 1955, a grand jury did not find Roy Bryant and J. W. Milam guilty of the kidnapping that they had acknowledged, and where in 2007, then in 2022, two other grand juries refused to pronounce new charges. The statue would have stood next to or replaced the monument already in that space, which is a gigantic statue that glorifies the defeated Confederates and commemorates the capture of the *Star of the West*, a Union ship that was transporting wounded troops in 1861, in what

EPILOGUE: THE STATUES' GAZE

is sometimes considered one of the first shots fired in the Civil War. Two years later, the Confederates scuttled the ship in the middle of the Tallahatchie River in a vain attempt to slow the advance of General Grant's troops.

In June 2020, the four Black members of the county council recommended the destruction of the Confederate statue—with the concession that no other statue be erected on the same site, not even to pay homage to those who had fought for civil rights. The only elected white person abstained from the vote, opposing the destruction.

Three years later, in summer 2023, the Confederate monument still stood. At its top, a general with a severe mustache holding artillery binoculars gazes at the building across the street where, in the 1950s, the White Citizens' Councils was headquartered—the organization of prominent citizens who made segregation reign through threats and intimidation. Staring at the statue, the Councils' founder and president, Robert Patterson, used to proclaim to anyone who would listen his determination not to "let the Yankees mongrelize us without protest."

In October 2022, given the lack of space in front of the courthouse, the decision was made to erect the statue of Emmett Till farther to the south, on a square along Johnson Street. In the past, this artery lined with worn storefronts had been known as a nightlife strip in Greenwood, and is where the young man spent the last evening of his life, having a good time.

Across the railroad tracks, stood Baptist Town, the old Black neighborhood; civil rights activists moved there en masse. On June 16, 1966, one of them named Stokely Carmichael waved a slogan that would take its place in history: BLACK POWER.

In the summer of 2023, a few yards from the statue on the same square, the town erected a sign to commemorate the life and work of a native of the area, playwright and activist Endesha Ida Mae Holland. On the sweaty afternoon of August 31, 1955, she was eleven years old and was playing behind a church in the neighborhood when they brought the body of Emmett Till, nibbled by fish, to the funeral home. The employee, a man who gave the full measure of his talent when he was a little drunk, searched through his cupboards to look for a little something to give him courage. With her friends, the little girl caught a glimpse of the victim's massacred head and exploded eyes before she was chased away by a group of white men. "Y'all see what kin happen when you sass-out white women?"

EPILOGUE: THE STATUES' GAZE

Almost seven decades later, Emmett Till, the teenager from Chicago, holds his head straight, and his eyes are wide open under his eternal fedora. The bronze has burnished his traits. It's easy to see the young man that he was, but also the adult and the friendly grandfather he could have been.

The day before the statue was dedicated, workers heaved it onto the pedestal by putting a rope around its neck. This time it was as if the old weapons of lynchings allowed his elevation. Standing five hundred yards from the courthouse, Emmett Till turns his back on the defeated Confederate general and gazes ahead into the distance.

APPENDICES

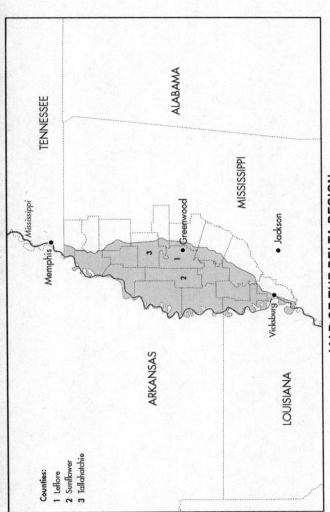

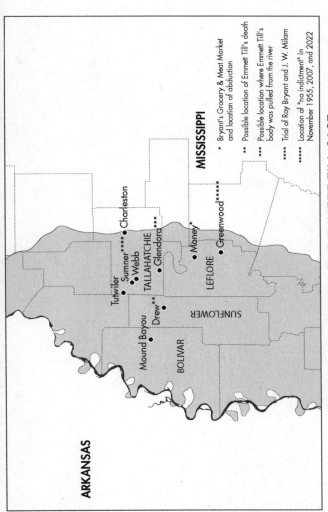

Chronology

November 23, 1921: Mamie Elizabeth Carthan is born in Webb, Mississippi.

January 1924: The family of Mamie Carthan moves from Mississippi to the suburbs of Chicago, Illinois.

July 25, 1941: Emmett Louis Till, son of Louis Till and Mamie Carthan, is born in Chicago.

May 17, 1954: The Supreme Court declares school segregation unconstitutional in *Brown v. Board of Education of Topeka, Kansas*.

May 7 and 13, 1955: George W. Lee and Lamar Smith, two African American activists, are killed in Mississippi. These are the first two murders classified as lynchings in the United States since 1951.

May 31, 1955: In its enforcement decree in *Brown v. Board of Education II*, the Supreme Court orders the states to proceed toward desegregation of public schools "with all deliberate speed."

August 24, 1955: An incident brings Emmett Till, on vacation for four days in Mississippi, into opposition with Carolyn Bryant, the grocer at Bryant's Grocery & Meat Market in Money, Mississippi.

August 28, 1955: Emmett Till is abducted from his great-uncle's house late at night by Roy Bryant, husband of Carolyn, and his half brother J. W. Milam.

August 31, 1955: The corpse of Emmett Till is found in the early morning by a fisherman in the Tallahatchie River, north of Money.

September 6, 1955: After four days of mourning followed by tens of thousands of Chicago residents, Emmett Till is buried in Alsip, in the southwest corner of greater Chicago. Roy Bryant and J. W. Milam are charged with kidnapping and murder by a grand jury of citizens of Tallahatchie County.

September 23, 1955: After a five-day trial, Roy Bryant and J. W. Milam are acquitted of the murder of Emmett Till by the Circuit Court of the Second District of Tallahatchie County.

October 14, 1955: The *Jackson Daily News* reveals that Louis Till, father of Emmett Till, was hanged for murder and rape in Italy in July 1945.

November 9, 1955: A grand jury of citizens of Leflore County refuses to charge Roy Bryant and J. W. Milam for the kidnapping of Emmett Till.

CHRONOLOGY

November 27, 1955: In the presence of Martin Luther King Jr. and Rosa Parks, Dr. T. R. M. Howard gives a speech on the murder of Emmett Till and civil rights in Mississippi at the Baptist Church on Dexter Avenue in Montgomery, Alabama. The Montgomery bus boycott starts one week later.

January 10, 1956: *Look* magazine publishes an article presented as Roy Bryant's and J. W. Milam's confessions of the murder of Emmett Till.

June 12, 1963: Medgar Evers is assassinated in Jackson, Mississippi.

August 1963: Hugh Stephen Whitaker, a student at Florida State University, defends his master's thesis written in the form of an investigation of the Emmett Till case.

August 28, 1963: Martin Luther King Jr. gives his "I Have a Dream" speech during the March on Washington for Jobs and Freedom.

June 21, 1964: In the case that will inspire the movie *Mississippi Burning*, James Chaney, Andrew Goodman, and Michael Schwerner, three civil rights activists, are kidnapped and executed by Ku Klux Klan militants near Philadelphia, in central Mississippi.

December 31, 1980: J. W. Milam dies at the age of sixty-two in Jackson, Mississippi.

May 20, 1985: First broadcasting of the documentary *The Murder and the Movement* on the Chicago local channel WMAQ-TV.

January 21, 1987: The first episode of the documentary series *Eyes on the Prize*, dedicated especially to the case of Emmett Till, is broadcasted.

February 5, 1994: The first conviction related to a cold case of the civil rights era in Mississippi: Byron De La Beckwith is found guilty of the murder of Medgar Evers.

September 1, 1994: Roy Bryant dies in Jackson, Mississippi, at the age of sixty-three.

November 16 and December 12, 2002: The documentary films *The Untold Story of Emmett Louis Till* by Keith Beauchamp and *The Murder of Emmett Till* by Stanley Nelson premier in New York City.

January 6, 2003: Mamie Till-Mobley dies in Chicago.

February 6, 2004: Activist Alvin Sykes, director Keith Beauchamp, and Simeon Wright, cousin of Emmett Till, plead in favor of reopening the case before representatives of the federal government, of the FBI, and of the Mississippi judiciary authorities, in Oxford.

May 10, 2004: The federal government announces that they are opening an investigation into the Emmett Till case.

June 1, 2005: The body of Emmett Till is exhumed for an autopsy.

February 23, 2007: After examining the FBI investigation, a grand jury of Leflore County citizens refuses to pronounce new charges in the Emmett Till case.

October 2, 2007: The citizens of Tallahatchie County apologize to the Till family for the events of 1955.

October 7, 2008: The Emmett Till Unsolved Civil Rights Crime Act, which reopens investigations of racist crimes linked to the civil rights movement, is signed into law.

January 31, 2017: Timothy Tyson's book *The Blood of Emmett Till* is released. It asserts that Carolyn Bryant had gone back on her version of the case.

July 12, 2018: The federal government officially opens a new investigation into the Emmett Till case after Timothy Tyson's revelations.

December 6, 2021: The federal government announces that the investigation is being closed without seeking charges at the federal level.

June 21, 2022: A small group of activists uncovers a warrant for arrest dated August 29, 1955, and bearing the name of Carolyn Bryant.

July 6 and December 3, 2022: Activist demonstrators demand the arrest of Carolyn Bryant in Raleigh, North Carolina, then in Bowling Green, Kentucky.

August 2022: A grand jury of Leflore County citizens again refuses to bring further charges in the Emmett Till case.

April 25, 2023: Carolyn Bryant dies in Westlake, Louisiana, at the age of eighty-eight.

July 25, 2023: President Joe Biden proclaims the establishment of a national monument in honor of Emmett Till and Mamie Till-Mobley in Mississippi and in Chicago.

Sources

This book is the result of on-the-ground reporting in Mississippi, Chicago, and Tallahassee in the summer of 2023, interviews with the actors, witnesses, and experts in the Emmett Till case, and an exploration of the abundant written and audiovisual traces that remain: books, press articles, academic studies, documentaries, investigative reports, and public and private archival materials.

The following people granted me an interview in the context of this work: Ollie Gordon, the Reverend Wheeler Parker Jr., and Priscilla Sterling, members of the Emmett Till family; Christopher Benson, coauthor of the biographies of Mamie Till-Mobley and Wheeler Parker; Jim Hood, attorney general for the state of Mississippi from 2004 to 2020; Jim M. Greenlee, United States attorney for the northern district of Mississippi from 2001 to 2010; Dale Killinger and Lent Rice, former FBI agents; Bobby Rush, US representative from

Illinois's first congressional district of Illinois from 1993 to 2023; Ted Shaw, president of the NAACP Legal Defense Fund from 2004 to 2008; Corey Weibel, former assistant to Alvin Sykes; Patrick Weems, executive director of the Emmett Till Interpretive Center; Johnny B. Thomas, mayor of the village of Glendora; Gloria Dickerson, founder and CEO of the Emmett Till Academy; Hermon Johnson, director of the Mound Bayou Museum of African American Culture and History; Gerald Chatham Jr. and Jak Smith, sons of the prosecutors in the trial of 1955; Dwight Vick, grandson of one of the jurors in the 1955 trial; documentary filmmakers Keith Beauchamp and Stanley Nelson; historians Devery Anderson, David Beito, Linda Royster Beito, Elliott Gorn, Davis Houck, and Dave Tell; journalists Jerry Mitchell, Rich Samuels, and Wright Thompson.

Books and monographs

The works listed below are those that contributed the most to this investigation, either generally or in specific passages.

Anderson, Devery S. *Emmett Till: The Murder That Shocked the World and Propelled the Civil Rights Movement.* University Press of Mississippi, 2015.

Beito, David T. and Linda Royster Beito. *Black Maverick: T. R. M. Howard's Fight for Civil Rights and Economic Power.* University of Illinois Press, 2009.

Blue, Bonnie. *Emmett Till's Secret Witness: FBI Confidential Source Speaks.* B. L. Richey Publishing, 2012.

SOURCES

Booker, Simeon. *Shocking the Conscience: A Reporter's Account of the Civil Rights Movement.* University Press of Mississippi, 2012.

Bryant, Carolyn. "I Am More Than a Wolf Whistle: The Story of Carolyn Bryant Donham as Written by Marsha Bryant." Unpublished manuscript, 2008.

Clay, Maude Schuyler. *Delta Land.* University Press of Mississippi, 1999.

Dodd, Monroe. *Pursuit of Truth: From Kansas City's Libraries, Alvin Sykes Plotted an Unlikely Course to Civil Rights History.* The Kansas City Public Library, 2014.

Else, Jon. *True South: Henry Hampton and "Eyes on the Prize," the Landmark Television Series That Reframed the Civil Rights Movement.* Viking, 2017.

Gorn, Elliott J. *Let the People See: The Story of Emmett Till.* Oxford University Press, 2018.

Hailman, John. *From Midnight to Guntown: True Crime Stories from a Federal Prosecutor in Mississippi.* University Press of Mississippi, 2013.

Hendrickson, Paul. *Sons of Mississippi: A Story of Race and Its Legacy.* Knopf, 2003.

Holland, Endesha Ida Mae. *From the Mississippi Delta: A Memoir.* Simon & Schuster, 1997.

Houck, Davis W. and Matthew A. Grindy. *Emmett Till and the Mississippi Press.* University Press of Mississippi, 2008.

Hudson-Weems, Clenora. *Emmett Till: The Sacrificial Lamb of the Civil Rights Movement.* Bedford Publishers, 1994.

Huie, William Bradford. *Wolf Whistle, and Other Stories.* Signet Books, 1959.

Johnson, Paul. *The Plot of Shame: US Military Executions in Europe During WWII.* Frontline Books, 2023.

Metress, Christopher (ed.). *The Lynching of Emmett Till: A Documentary Narrative.* University of Virginia Press, 2002.

Mitchell, Jerry. *Race Against Time: A Reporter Reopens the Unsolved Murder Cases of the Civil Rights Era.* Simon & Schuster, 2020.

Neiman, Susan. *Learning from the Germans: Race and the Memory of Evil.* Farrar, Straus and Giroux, 2019.

Parker, Reverend Wheeler, Jr. and Christopher Benson. *A Few Days Full of Trouble: Revelations on the Journey to Justice for My Cousin and Best Friend, Emmett Till.* One World, 2023.

Roberts, Gene and Hank Klibanoff. *The Race Beat: The Press, the Civil Rights Struggle, and the Awakening of a Nation.* Knopf, 2006.

Romano, Renee C. *Racial Reckoning: Prosecuting America's Civil Rights Murders.* Harvard University Press, 2014.

Tell, Dave. *Remembering Emmett Till.* University of Chicago Press, 2019.

Theoharis, Jeanne. *The Rebellious Life of Mrs. Rosa Parks.* Beacon Press, 2013.

Thomas, Johnny B. and Thomas J. Durant Jr. *A Stone of Hope: Rising Above Slavery, Jim Crow, and Poverty in Glendora, Mississippi.* Xlibris, 2017.

Till-Mobley, Mamie and Christopher Benson. *Death of Innocence: The Story of the Hate Crime That Changed America*. Random House, 2003.

Tyson, Timothy B. *The Blood of Emmett Till*. Simon & Schuster, 2017.

Whitaker, Hugh Stephen. "A Case Study in Southern Justice: The Emmett Till Case," master's thesis. Florida State University, 1963.

Whitfield, Stephen J. *A Death in the Delta: The Story of Emmett Till*. Free Press, 1988.

Wideman, John Edgar. *Writing to Save a Life: The Louis Till File*. Scribner, 2016.

Wright, Simeon and Herb Boyd. *Simeon's Story: An Eyewitness Account of the Kidnapping of Emmett Till*. Chicago Review Press, 2010.

Press

The press was especially helpful to me in reconstructing the events of the period. First and foremost were the daily newspapers, such as *The Atlanta Journal-Constitution*, the *Chicago Tribune*, *The Clarion-Ledger*, *The Commercial Appeal*, *Delta Democrat Times*, *The Greenwood Commonwealth*, *Jackson Daily News*, *The New York Times*, dispatches of the Associated Press, and the work of the Mississippi Center for Investigative Reporting. There were also weekly papers and magazines, including *Baltimore Afro-American*, *The Chicago Defender*, *Ebony*, and *Jet*. The articles below were particularly valuable to this project with their exclusive news and commentaries.

Anonymous (Editorial). "Emmett Till, and Mamie Till-Mobley, Still Await Justice." *Chicago Tribune,* July 17, 2022.

Atkins, Joe and Tom Brennan. "Bryant Wants the Past to 'Stay Dead.'" *The Clarion-Ledger*, August 25, 1985.

Bartlow Martin, John. "The Deep South Says, 'Never!'" *The Saturday Evening Post*, June 29, 1957.

Browning, William. "Till Jury Talks: Grand Jury Says Evidence Wasn't There to Indict." *The Greenwood Commonwealth*, September 30, 2007.

Darden, Bob. "Chiles Says Citizens Must Get Involved to Fight Crime." *The Greenwood Commonwealth*, September 16, 2004.

Hicks, James L. "Unbelievable! Jimmy Hicks' Inside Story of Lynch Trial." *The Baltimore Afro-American*, October 8, 1955.

Holmberg, David. "The Legacy of Emmett Till." *The Palm Beach Post*, September 4, 1994.

Huie, William Bradford. "The Shocking Story of an Approved Killing in Mississippi." *Look*, January 24, 1956.

Huie, William Bradford. "What's Happened to the Emmett Till Killers." *Look*, January 22, 1957.

Lewis, John. "Together, You Can Redeem the Soul of Our Nation." *The New York Times*, July 30, 2020.

Thompson, Wright. "His Name Was Emmett Till." *The Atlantic*, September 2021.

Wakefield, Dan. "Justice in Sumner." *The Nation*, October 1955.

Weller, Sheila. "How Author Timothy Tyson Found the Woman at the Center of the Emmett Till Case." *Vanity Fair*, January 26, 2017.

Wright, Mose. "I Saw Them Take Emmett Till." *Front Page Detective*, February 1956.

Fictional works

Women of the Movement, a series created for ABC by Marissa Jo Cerar, 2022.

Till, a film directed by Chinonye Chukwu, 2022.

Television and radio documentaries

The Murder and the Movement (WMAQ-TV, 1985)

Eyes on the Prize: America's Civil Rights Movement (Blackside, 1987–1990)

The Murder of Emmett Till (Plater Robinson and Loretta Williams, 1996)

The Murder of Emmett Till (Stanley Nelson, 2003)

The Untold Story of Emmett Louis Till (Keith Beauchamp, 2005)

The Lost Story of Emmett Till (NBC Chicago, 2022)

Let the World See (ABC, 2022)

Acknowledgments

First of all, a huge thank-you to all the people mentioned in the preceding pages who agreed to talk to me about the Emmett Till case and share their memories and analyses with generosity and a sense of warm welcome, from Chicago to Mississippi, by way of Florida or from a distance.

Thanks also to those who helped me by facilitating interviews or reports, by clarifying details or sharing documents, especially Marvel Parker of the Emmett Till & Mamie Till-Mobley Institute, journalist Joe Atkins, photographer Mark Mirko, Beverly Pettigrew Kraft of the Administrative Office of Courts of the State of Mississippi, Charles Diaz and Hélène Chaulin of the American Battle Monuments Commission, and

Jeff Andrews. Thanks also for the help offered by the archivists at the Carter G. Woodson Regional Library in Chicago, the Mississippi Department of Archives and History in Jackson, and the Claude Pepper Library at Florida State University in Tallahassee.

Thanks to Mark H'Limi and Sulivan Clabaut for teaching me how to talk about American criminal histories into a microphone before I wrote one myself, and to my predecessors in this series, Arthur Cerf, Thibault Raisse, Anaïs Renevier, and William Thorp, for our discussions relating to their books which, I hope, have contributed to making this one better.

Special thanks, finally, to my family and friends for encouraging me in the idea for this book, as well as Elsa Delachair and Stéphane Régy for their confidence and their assistance throughout this project.

About the Author

Jean-Marie Pottier was born in Rennes (in western France) in 1982. He works as a reporter for the French social sciences monthly *Sciences humaines*, and contributes to the ARTE series *Le Dessous des images*, to the history online magazine *Retronews*, and to the pop-music magazine *Magic*. He has written many stories on American society and culture, especially for the French version of the online magazine *Slate*, of which he is the former editor in chief, and for the bimonthly *Society*. He has also published several books in French about American music for the publisher Le mot et le reste, most notably *Ground Zero. Une histoire musicale du 11-Septembre* (2016) and *Alternative nation. La scène indépendante américaine 1979-2001* (2021).